# Nerds Rednecks & Knuckleheads

Jeff Maskevich

Nerds Rednecks & Knuckleheads

Text © Jeff Maskevich, 2020

Cover by BEAUTeBOOK, 2020

Published by River Birch Press
P.O. Box 868
Daphne, Alabama 36526

The author asserts the moral right under the Copyright, Designs and Patents Act of 1988 to be identified as the author of this work.

All Rights reserved. With the exception of brief excerpts as part of a published review, no part of this publication may be reproduced, stored in a retrieval system, or transmitted, in any form or by any means without the prior written consent of the author, nor be otherwise circulated in any form of binding or cover other than that in which it is published and without a similar condition being imposed on the subsequent purchaser.

# Table of Contents

Chapter 1
Knucklehead Breakthrough ................................................. 11

Chapter 2
A Redneck with Wheels ...................................................... 21

Chapter 3
The Kingdom of God Disguised as Camp Snoopy ......... 29

Chapter 4
Guilt on the Rocks ............................................................... 43

Chapter 5
Criminal Thinking Error #8 ................................................ 53

Chapter 6
Job is Not a Republican ...................................................... 61

Chapter 7
A Deaf Man Hears from God ............................................. 75

Chapter 8
Here is Grace ........................................................................ 85

Chapter 9
The Blessing of Fear ............................................................ 95

Chapter 10
Bad Credit? No Credit? No Problem! ............................. 111

Chapter 11
Discipleship Happens ....................................................... 123

Chapter 12
Let the Chunks Fall Where They May ........................... 143

# Introduction

**Concerning Rednecks...**

Rednecks come in all assortments. You've got your hicks, your hayseeds, and your hillbillies, depending on your location. In my neck of the woods, most hicks, hayseeds, and hillbillies look the part.

I think there are more rednecks out there than we realize (try saying that like Andy Rooney).

My friend Kathie is a redneck. I wasn't entirely sure, so I asked her. I had to ask because she doesn't look like a redneck. All her shirts have sleeves. When she asked me what kind of redneck she was, I told her she was an incognito redneck. That's because no one would ever suspect she's a redneck just by looking at her.

I think being a redneck is more about the state of mind and less about the appearance. If you're comfortable knowing:

God is smarter than you
Common sense isn't offensive
It's okay to wear camo pajama bottoms at home (but not at Walmart)

then chances are, you've got some redneck DNA.

I have redneck sons. I'll be honest; I never expected to have redneck kids. When I watched them, I always asked myself this question: *Am I as much a redneck as these little nerds?*

How much of a redneck was I? I didn't even know I was a redneck until I saw my redneck DNA in my own kids.

I'll credit my friend Greg with enlightening me. One day he just came straight out and told me I was I redneck. (This probably won't be news to my friends.) He said my kids got their redneckedness from me. Since this news came from Greg, I believed it. He gets a handle on people pretty quickly. I'm grateful he helped me identify my inner redneck.

I'm over myself now.

Hi. I'm Jeff. I'm a redneck.

Hi, Jeff.

I'm writing this book for rednecks because I know my audience.

**Concerning Nerds...**

It doesn't take one to know one. But it doesn't hurt either.

I'm also a nerd. I have Hogwarts pajama bottoms. And a Gryffindor scarf. Just bragging about this stuff makes me a nerd. (I just now figured that out ... more confirmation.)

Anything less than the extended version of the Lord of the Rings is not up to par.

My car advertises my nerdiness. My rear-window sticker announces my graduation from Starfleet Academy. I have a Hogwarts Express 9 ¾ sticker on my side window. Plus a "Fellowship of the Ring" silhouette sticker with Gandalf the Grey leading the way.

I can quote from every Star Trek movie. Except *Star Trek: Nemesis*. That wouldn't be cool.

As with my redneck discovery, I did not learn of my nerdiness until much later in life. Evidently self-discovery isn't all that easy for nerds and rednecks. At least it wasn't for this one.

I know rednecks. I know nerds.

**Concerning Knuckleheads...**

I'll just let Google sum it up for you...

> knuck.le.head / 'nukul,hed /
> Noun informal 1. a stupid person

We are not all rednecks. We are not all nerds. But no one is immune from being a knucklehead from time to time.

If you are a nerd or a redneck, you'll probably relate to my stories. If you're a knucklehead, don't worry. I tried to use small words.

Whether you're a nerd, redneck, or knucklehead, I want to minister to you through this book. Churchgoer or not.

This book shoots straight. It's about supernatural things I witnessed God doing. Things about His Kingdom, and what happened when I simply spoke God's message in plain language.

Sadly, from what I can tell, preachers have been talking over folks' heads for years. They assume folks know more about God's Kingdom than they let on.

That's a problem.

In our day and age, the church isn't the kind of place that helps people to ask questions about spiritual things they don't understand. I even know church leaders who are afraid to be spiritually curious. Too many church folk are afraid to ask a question or give an answer out of fear of sounding stupid.

Not to mention pat answers to deep and difficult questions.

So I figured enough is enough. I'm going to write about Jesus and His Kingdom in plain language. Simple and honest answers for everyday folks.

At the end of my personal stories, I'll connect a few spiritual dots between the stories and what the Bible says. This is a bonus for all you nerds, rednecks, and knuckleheads who never felt comfortable asking questions at church.

These chapters are mini-chapters of ministry in my life. My stories might be worded in plain language, but the Kingdom lessons are rich and deep. I'm guessing you may even find a few nuggets of your own.

This book is a chapter too. It's the chapter of my life, in which I get to connect the dots. Many at one time, for lots of everyday folks all at once.

People, even rednecks, are important to me. I think that will become clear to you as you read these stories.

"I don't know half of you half as well as I should like, and I like less than half of you half as well as you deserve." This is for you.

# Preface

Dear Nerd, Redneck, and/or Knucklehead,

The main reason I wrote this book was to brag on God—to brag on His grace and the glory His grace brings Him—all against the backdrop of our knuckleheadedness. If there is one thing I would like you to see as you go through these pages is my boasting in the Lord.

I have included no stories about "biblical knuckleheads" in these pages. The stories deal with local knuckleheads only and involve infamous murderers, pregnant teen-age girls, death bed confessions, and supernatural conversions in the Haitian jungle.

But *If I were* to choose a knucklehead from the Bible to write about, it would be Jonah. Jonah's story was not really about a soggy knucklehead but rather about God and His grace.

Even after being graciously deposited on the shore, instead of being digested, Jonah still had trouble connecting the dots of God's deliverance. We are in the same company as Jonah.

The Bible often makes comparisons between God and us. First Corinthians 1:25 says, "The foolishness of God is wiser than human wisdom, and the weakness of God is stronger than human strength."

The reason man's "wisdom" and "strength" have quotations around them is because like Jonah, we are neither wise or strong. If you want proof you can either watch FAIL ARMY on YouTube or read the Bible.

When I write about the highlights and lowlights of

nerds, rednecks, and knuckleheads, I write from experience—theirs and mine. While there are plenty of them written about in this book, it's not so much a story about them. Like Jonah's story, it's about God and how He uses His sovereign grace to fit us into *His* story despite *our* wisdom and strength.

This being said, I would like to connect a couple of dots.

- "Brothers, think of what you were when you were called. Not many of you were wise by human standards. Not many were influential. Not many of us were from noble birth. He chose the lowly things, and the despised things – and the things that are not – to nullify the things that are, so that no one may boast before him." (1 Corinthians 1:26-29)

- Han Solo had it right. Don't get cocky kid.

- *"It is because of him* that you are in Christ Jesus, who has become for us the wisdom of God—that is our righteousness, holiness and redemption. Therefore, as it is written: "Let him who boasts boast in the Lord. (1 Corinthians 1:30-31)

# Chapter 1
# Knucklehead Breakthrough

Jesus wrote a blank check, one I hadn't cashed yet. My Heavenly account wasn't paid in full until I was thirty-one. Until then, I had no idea I was bouncing checks to the Almighty.

The Lithuanian Catholic church I grew up in was extremely ornate. Even the bathrooms were holy. It was all so beautiful. Statues. Stained glass. Lots of candles. Angels painted on the ceiling. It also smelled like incense. Patchouli, I think. Incense was used to carry your prayers to God. I always wondered why God needed patchouli.

That was my idea of church.

My mother, the godliest person I've ever known, cried when they tore down that church building. It bugged me too.

But when I was converted, I wasn't surrounded by gold foil lettering inscribed on marble altars. The church where I was converted had brown paneling.

The first time I walked in, I almost turned around and walked out. From my understanding, if it didn't look religious, then it must not be. But at the time, my spiritual perspective was like looking through a pea shooter. Pretty narrow. Where was the altar? The angels? My patchouli? This place smelled more like Pine-Sol. But brown paneling? Seriously? I had a hard time with that. I wasn't sure how God felt about 1/8-inch decorative plywood in a sanctuary.

When it came to spiritual temples, I lived a pretty sheltered life. I did, however, attend a Lutheran church once when I was a sophomore in high school. I went with my girlfriend. I don't think I can count that because all I remember thinking was, *Where are we going to make out after this service?* Even so, the Lutherans didn't impress me either.

The church folk with the paneling, however? They were quite friendly. They didn't judge this scruffy-looking renegade with a rock-and-roll attitude. They were solid. Graceful. Accepting. Not only the building, but the people also taught me that God looks at the inside. That's me connecting the dots, maybe for the first time.

God used a teenaged girl, a neighbor of ours who babysat our kids for us, to invite our family to the brown-paneled church. It was 1991 and I was thirty-two at the time. Carrie and I had two sons, Maxwell and Alex. We took her up on her invitation, put on our finest polyester, and braved going to church with the kids.

Pastor Rick gave us a short tour of the church when we got there. Being raised Catholic, I had never seen a knee-deep baptistery before. A couple hundred gallons instead of a pint? That's odd. The mold around the baptistery walls confused me too. Aren't churches supposed to be ultra-sterile? You know—holy? Like my former temple?

But I rolled with it. The folks there were down to earth. Their genuine friendliness made it easy to overlook what I did not understand.

After that first service, Pastor Rick invited Carrie and

me over to his house. He wasted no time sharing that Jesus died to pay our debt to God. To forgive our guilty souls. And Heaven everlasting would be our reward! He told us straight up: we must accept Jesus by faith.

Wow, ten years an altar boy and I don't remember hearing that message. I know this may sound incredible, but I was spiritually brain dead.

There were plenty of spiritual traps to get in a young altar boy's way. What's black and white and red all over? An embarrassed altar boy who tripped on his cassock and fell in front of the entire parish. Yep, yours truly. How about the time another altar boy spilled the communion wine during Mass? He's still doing penance. Even with all the statues, it never felt like a very spiritual place. Possibly because the church janitor always wanted to show us boys his newest issue of *Playboy*.

I served Mass hundreds of times. Not once did that priest ever speak to me about anything spiritual. All in all, my first temple was not a very spiritual place.

That evening at Pastor Rick's house, he got right to the gospel. My wife listened to him tell us that God forgives sinners, and she believed right then and there. God was quick with Carrie. She had a jump on me, though. She never had to clean communion wine out of the church carpet. Or explain to her parents where those *Playboy* centerfolds came from.

I had baggage. I was skeptical about Jesus. Pastor Rick from the church of the brown paneling was okay with that. We agreed to meet every week. I had no idea he was evangelizing. I never felt like Rick was trying to rush me into a fraternity. The guy was simply my new pal.

After meeting with Rick a few times and hearing from him that Jesus was God in the flesh, I did not want anything to do with Jesus. What heresy! Jesus is God? I'd never heard that one before.

Actually, I had heard it before. Hundreds of times growing up in the beautiful church. But it never registered.

How's that for being a spiritual knucklehead? Sheesh! My spiritual porch light was on, but nobody was home. I thought Rick had screws loose and wires crossed. Of course, I was an expert on religion, don't you know? After all, I did have my opinions.

It seems anyone who has a spiritual opinion is an expert on spirituality. Myself included.

Instead of trying to persuade me or argue with me, Rick let God do the work. Rick was my guide, but God converted me through His Spirit and Word. Pastor Rick's patience and gentleness with me would deeply impact how I would eventually evangelize others.

Rick had me read through the book of John. That's a good starting place for a guy who doesn't believe Jesus is God. God dealt with me rather effectively. I just needed Someone (that's a capital S) to point me in the right direction.

I sat down one night and read about seven chapters of John. I went to Rick's office the next week and argued with him some more about Jesus. Then I read a few more chapters. Then argued with Rick again.

But when I got to John 16:7, I heard Jesus say, "Unless I go away the 'Counselor' will not come." "Who is this Counselor?" I asked Rick. When he told me this

Counselor was the Holy Spirit, I immediately believed. I got it. Converted! Turned on a dime. Jesus cashed my blank check. Only then did figure out I was flat broke.

God made good on what I could not. Jesus gave me grace from His cross. Not only did He forgive me, but He gave me the precious gift of faith as well. A direct deposit right into my heavenly bank account. No way that check could ever bounce. His promise. His blood. His life. His resurrection. His Spirit. These are my spiritual collateral.

It's amazing what God's Word can do. Just like when He spoke the world into existence. From complete darkness He created light, simply by His words. When He converted me, He used His words—specifically the words of John from the Bible. Just like creating something from nothing, He made a spiritually dead redneck, an angry rock-and-roller, believe.

Later, Pastor Rick baptized me in that moldy tub. Only the three of us were there, though: Rick, me, and God. I admit it. At that time I was too self-conscious to proclaim Christ in front of anybody else.

I'll never forget driving down the street afterward and feeling really clean after sliding around in that grungy baptistery.

I am grateful to Pastor Rick. He spoke the truth to me in love.

Later Pastor Rick would leave the brown-paneled church. His exit was harsh and painful. I watched him be sabotaged like Jesus. His faithfulness and zeal to proclaim Jesus and His cross gave me a pattern to follow. I wanted to be like Pastor Rick. Gutsy and proud of the gospel.

It didn't take long for me to start telling people about Jesus and His gospel. Now the hard part is getting me to shut up.

The Counselor gave me confidence in Jesus. He alone made me right with Him, and it changed the course of my life. There is no way I can repay Him. So I will enjoy Him.

From a guy who was shy at his baptism, I've turned a one-eighty.

Today, one of my favorite ways to enjoy Him is to tell others about Him. I've always loved singing this hymn. It describes my passion for Jesus and His gospel.

> *I love to tell the story of unseen things above,*
> *Of Jesus and His glory, of Jesus and His love;*
> *I love to tell the story, because I know 'tis true,*
> *It satisfies my longings as nothing else would do.*
>
> *I love to tell the story,*
> *'Twill be my theme in glory,*
> *To tell the old, old story*
> *Of Jesus and His love.*
>
> *I love to tell the story, more wonderful it seems*
> *Than all the golden fancies of all our golden dreams;*
> *I love to tell the story, it did so much for me,*
> *And that is just the reason I tell it now to thee.*
>
> *I love to tell the story, 'tis pleasant to repeat,*
> *What seems each time I tell it more wonderfully sweet;*
> *I love to tell the story, for some have never heard*
> *The message of salvation from God's own holy Word.*
>
> *I love to tell the story, for those who know it best*
> *Seem hungering and thirsting to hear it like the rest;*

*And when in scenes of glory I sing the new, new song,
'Twill be the old, old story that I have loved so long.*

He wrote me a blank check. Filled in the necessary amount. Deposited it into my heavenly bank account. Ka-ching, He cashed it. Then He did me one better. He let me invest in some other folks' heavenly bank accounts.

The stories you will read in the pages ahead are all about Jesus and His sovereign grace. The players are nerds, rednecks, knuckleheads, and God. Much like the gospel stories, they all start and end with Jesus.

I didn't know it then, and it took me some time to figure it out, but something larger than my personal salvation was at work.

## *Connecting the Dots*

- How could I be spiritually blind and deaf to the gospel after hearing it all those years as I grew up in the church?

- The god of this age [Satan] has blinded the minds of unbelievers, so that they cannot see the light of the gospel of the glory of Christ, who is the image of God. (2 Corinthians 4:4 NIV)

- Like the blind we grope along the wall, feeling our way like people without eyes. At midday we stumble as if it were twilight; among the strong, we are like the dead. (Isaiah 59:10 NIV)

- As for you, you were dead in your transgressions and sins. (Ephesians 2:1 NIV)

- The heart is deceitful above all things and beyond cure. Who can understand it? (Jeremiah 17:9 NIV)

- To this John [the Baptist] replied, "A person can receive only what is given him from Heaven." (John 3:27 NIV)

- God used His Spirit and His Word (the Bible) not just to reveal Himself to me, but to redeem my soul.

- For you have been born again, not of perishable seed, but of imperishable, through the living and enduring word of God. (1 Peter 1:23 NIV)

- And you also were included in Christ when you heard the message of truth, the gospel of your salvation.

When you believed, you were marked in him with a seal, the promised Holy Spirit, who is a deposit guaranteeing our inheritance until the redemption of those who are God's possession—to the praise of his glory. (Ephesians 1:13-14 NIV)

- His blank check was backed up with the blood of Christ.
- "For you know that it was not with perishable things such as silver or gold that you were redeemed from the empty way of life handed down to you from your ancestors, but with the precious blood of Christ, a lamb without blemish or defect." (1 Peter 1:18-19 NIV)

- There is more to being a Christian than salvation. Not only did He breathe life into me to create my faith, but He uses His life to perfect my faith as well. When I look at the path of my Lord and I am told to follow Him, I have to expect my path will be gut-wrenching, just as His was.
- "Let us fix our eyes on Jesus, the author and perfecter of faith, who for the joy that was set before him he endured the cross, scorning its shame, and sat down at the right hand of the throne of God." (Hebrews 12:2)

God used nerds, rednecks, and knuckleheads to break through to one of their own. To tell me His story. To show me His plan. Now I'm able to tell His story to others. This book is a natural overflow of His love expressed to me.

Remember… "You are the light of the world. A town built on a hill cannot be hidden. Neither do people light a lamp and put it under a bowl. Instead they put it on its stand, and it gives light to everyone in the house. In the same way, let your light shine before others, that they may see your good deeds and glorify your Father in Heaven." (Matthew 5:14-16 NIV)

## Chapter 2
## A Redneck with Wheels

Carl had just gotten out of prison for conspiracy to commit murder. He was a nice guy for a convicted felon. Turns out he tried selling a gun to an undercover police officer, who then contacted the FBI.

When the FBI followed him, they noticed the "equipment" in the back seat of his car. The undercover FBI guys posing as fellow rednecks stopped Carl and asked to do business with him. Carl got really excited. Being the knucklehead he was, he eagerly agreed. Sorry, Carl. No one ever said you were the sharpest knife in the drawer.

During five years in federal prison, Carl spent a lot of time reading his Bible. When we met after his release, we soon discovered we spoke the same languages. Redneck and Bible.

A week before my ordination service, I started having conversations with Carl, my new ex-con friend.

As we talked, he showed me some things about God I did not expect. Yes, I was being ordained, but I wasn't so knowledgeable that I couldn't learn something new about the Bible from an ex-con.

It's not every day that a man convicted of conspiracy to commit murder informs you that God chose you and that you did not choose Him. Hmm? Okay, I'll bite. Carl had me read some Bible passages about God's electing grace. Ephesians 1:4 got me thinking: "For he chose us in him before the creation of the world to be holy and blameless in his sight (NIV)."

I didn't immediately believe Carl when he said God had picked me. Can you blame me? I could have sworn I chose Jesus all by myself. God choosing knuckleheads is not logical. But I was starting to learn about the "logic" of grace.

When I was growing up, the priest never told us altar boys about God's choosing. Plus, I was about to be ordained in a church where the mere mention of the word election got you some strange looks. It takes time to figure out church.

I was eager to learn about God. So I read. I began to notice some patterns about God choosing folks. What better place to bring my newfound observations about God's election than to my Sunday school class? And who better to ask than the wife of one of the elders?

I showed up to Sunday school, all eager to be enlightened. I asked my questions from my heart, out of genuine ignorance and innocence.

I asked, "I was reading and it looked as if God elected the prophets. Did God choose them? And then it looks like He chose Israel from all the other nations. And didn't God choose Joseph, Mary's husband? What about Moses? Was that a chance meeting? And then my friend Carl had me reading Ephesians, and it says God chose me too. Am I reading all this stuff correctly?"

This kindhearted elder's wife—who always smiled—looked at me with her face all twisted up. She looked as if she had just smelled Jonah after he was puked up on the shore. She rolled her eyes and asked, "You're not a Calvinist, are you?"

"Calvinist? What's a Calvinist?" Whatever it was, I

could tell I shouldn't be one. I walked away confused.

I think what happened to me happens to a lot of people. You ask a question in church. The answer, if you get one, makes you feel stupid. So from that point on, you pretend to know or you just agree with everything that's said.

Or you stop going altogether.

I asked our new pastor to connect the theological dots for me. By this time, Pastor Rick had moved on. The new minister quickly told me that our church doesn't promote that kind of teaching. At this church, the subject of God's election—Him choosing me—was not a main course on their menu. In fact, it wasn't even an appetizer. I understood where they were coming from.

Then the subject changed. The new pastor asked who would give me my "charge" at my ordination service. (A charge is a short message aimed at the new minister, instructing him to go and preach the gospel). I told him it would be Carl. And by the providence of God, my new pastor agreed. Funny how that works. Don't let anyone tell you God doesn't have a sense of humor.

Carl did a good job giving me my charge. Sort of. I'll never forget the wry, crooked smile on his face as he preached to me. He knew my church didn't emphasize election. Yet Carl didn't hold back the snickers and nods he aimed at me. Election. God's choosing. God chose you, buddy. Now go and do His bidding. Know what I mean? Wink, wink. Nudge, nudge.

Dang it, Carl. That wasn't nice.

Even though he was a federal felon and made fun of my church's beliefs in front of my family, friends, and that elder's wife, I was becoming more convinced that Carl and the Bible were right. A convicted knuckleheaded redneck felon versus the Sunday school teacher/elder's wife? Hmm.

A spiritual line was drawn for me.

At the time of my ordination, I was doing jail ministry. Carl had introduced me to Dave, who had ministered to him while he was doing time in the federal pen.

Dave was an older pastor who had been teaching inmates in the prison system for years. I was only in jail ministry and I wanted to "move up" to the big house. In my thinking, moving from jail ministry to prison ministry would be like a spiritual promotion.

Dave invited me to a Prison Fellowship weekend seminar. Prison Fellowship was founded by the late Chuck Colson—a great training ground for me. So I went with PF to a large, high-security prison on the plains of Colorado. How could I say no?

Dave was a wonderful teacher. Brilliant, actually. His sermons to the inmates were captivating. Dave was clear and passionate. There are a lot of redneck Christians in prison, so when it was my turn to teach, I felt quite at home. We spoke the same language. More Bible and redneck. Listening to Dave and preaching the gospel was OJT (on-the-job training).

After that first day of teaching, our team went back to the motel for dinner. Dave invited me to dig deeper into the Bible. And what did we talk about? Election. Dave pointed me to John 3:8: "The wind blows wherever it pleases. You hear its sound, but you cannot tell where it comes from or where it is going. So it is with everyone born of the Spirit."

So that's how somebody gets saved? It's by the Holy Spirit? Wow! This was incredible. It was actually God who saves sinners. God saved me. Hey, wait a minute ... I'm a knucklehead. You mean I didn't do this? Wait another minute. I couldn't have done this. Grace was sinking in.

I was a Christian, all right. But I was learning more about another sparkling facet of God's grace. Grace like a diamond.

I remember going back to my motel room and crying. Crying hard. Crying because God chose me. Oh, my goodness. How could this be? The revelation brought me to my knees. God chose me, stupid redneck Jeff. I cried. I worshipped. I was humbled. This truth, this grace, about what God did for me forever changed the way I see God and others and myself.

The next day, we went into the prison with the rest of the volunteer team. One of the volunteers—there's no other way to put this—was a loudmouthed jerk. A doctrinal spiritual know-it-all who no one wanted to be around.

I got stuck in the sally port with this guy. The sally port is the small area where you wait for the gate in front of you to open while the gate behind you closes. The guards must have been doing something important, like getting coffee, because we had to wait in the sally port for about ten minutes. I was cornered. All I could think was, "Don't make eye contact."

Then this guy started to grill me on election. Really? Election again? Eventually, he asked me if God chose me or if I chose God. Wow. Apparently this is a hot topic with a lot of folks. Still feeling the power of the previous night's revelation, I said in a low, steady voice, "That's right. I believe God chose me." But I wanted to shout, "Hey, man! My God chose me, knucklehead Jeff. How do you like that, you arrogant jerk? Oh, and one more thing. Keep your pie hole shut about election." But I didn't shout or say any of those things. I was cool. I was calm. Shouting is never good in prison ministry.

I guess the combination of my self-control and firmly held theology started to annoy him. He got so upset with me, he didn't let up until we got to the area where we would teach the inmates. I just let him blow. You have to keep your cool in prison ministry. There was no way I was going to get into another bout over election.

At that moment, I knew what I believed. I had spiritually connected the dots.

I guess he had enough of me, because when we got to the seminar, he told the correctional officers that he had to leave the facility. Which was a bummer, since he had brought the cookies and Kool-Aid.

God's election is not well received by some people. I think folks believe it makes God look unfair, and they don't like it. And I get that. That's what the guy with the Kool-Aid thought.

God deals with each of us individually. And He is never unjust. God chooses sinners. That's grace.

I believe the Bible is clear. Through His election before the world was created, God promises to save sinners. He chose me before I could believe and be forgiven. This shows me just how bad my sin is. And His election proves how amazing His grace is.

## *Connecting the Dots*

Sovereign grace to undeserving sinners proves God is love.

- God elects and predestines knuckleheads to receive His grace. He even arranges "chance" meetings between guys like me and Carl. This is sovereign grace. I cannot explain it. I can only marvel at His providence.

- And we know that in all things God works for the good of those who love him, who have been called according to his purpose. For those God foreknew he also predestined to be conformed to the image of his Son. (Romans 8:28-29 NIV)

- I thank God (and the FBI) for arresting Carl so I could end up seeing what God did for me. And to keep the streets safe. He does indeed work together strange things with strange people. Thank You, Lord, for Carl the redneck. God wanted me to know He is responsible for my belief in Him.

- Yet to all who did receive him, to those who believed in his name, he gave the right to become children of God—children born not of natural descent, nor of human decision or a husband's will, but born of God. (John 1:12-13 NIV)

- [Jesus praying to the Father] "I have revealed you to those whom you gave me out of the world. They were yours; you gave them to me and they have obeyed your word." (John 17:6 NIV)

- When the Gentiles heard this, they were glad and honored the word of the Lord; and all who were appointed for eternal life believed. (Acts 13:48 NIV)

- "For he chose us in him before the creation of the world to be holy and blameless in his sight. In love he predestined us for adoption to sonship through Jesus Christ, in accordance with his pleasure and will—to the praise of his glorious grace, which he has freely given us in the One he loves." (Ephesians 1:4-6 NIV)

- Who is responsible for the salvation of your soul? My soul? Clearly it is God and His intentional grace.

I marvel at these Bible verses. It is one thing to know I am a Christian. It's something more to know how I became a Christian. To grasp the revelation that God chose me, and not the other way around, is both humbling and motivating.

People must be told. This is news! Really good news.

"The Kingdom of Heaven is like treasure hidden in a field. When a man found it, he hid it again, and then in his joy went and sold all he had and bought that field" (Matthew 13:44 NIV).

That man in the field? That's me.

Now I'm a redneck with wheels! *Aaaaaand* we're off...

# Chapter 3
# The Kingdom of God Disguised as Camp Snoopy

Mike called me from jail, asking me to bring his personal items. He knew he would be going away for a while—sixteen years.

Mike and I were best of pals. I knew about his secret sin. I didn't take his sin seriously enough. Obviously, neither did he.

I visited him in the county jail, and we talked on the phone. The one through the glass. A guy I worked with at the time said that I didn't have to see my pal through the glass. He said I could see him in person if I went into the jail with him through a Prison Fellowship Bible study. That was a no-brainer for me. I wanted to see my friend, so that's what I did.

For the next six months, I saw Mike once a week in the jail Bible study. That's how I eventually got called to prison ministry—by visiting my buddy Mike at the local jail.

After his sentencing, they locked him away in the state penitentiary. Meanwhile, I continued the jail ministry. God would convict both of us, each in our own context. A double conviction. Mike's heart. My call. A triple conviction if you count the state convicting Mike of his crime.

I ministered inside that jail as if I lived there. I told men the gospel. I counseled from the heart of the gospel. Eventually, I wanted to become a chaplain in the state prison system, and this required experience and ordination. When I approached the elders of the brown-paneled church, their response was simple: "Prove yourself."

So I did. I spent the next five years in jail ... ministry.

Mike and I stayed connected through writing letters. We branched off in different directions within the correctional system. Jail ministry for me. Hard time for Mike. While Mike was learning about con games and convicts behind the walls, I was learning about them in the Department of Corrections Training Academy.

After my academy training, Carrie and I sold our home and moved near the prison. I went full-time as a volunteer prison chaplain for the state of Colorado. Since it was not a paying gig, it mostly brought out chaplains who were serious about proclaiming the gospel. By law we were not allowed to proselytize (preach the gospel). Yeah, right. Like I wouldn't do that.

It took me longer than Mike, but after five years in jail ministry I ended up in prison ... ministry.

Actually, I never considered myself a prison chaplain. One time, I heard the head of Colorado Prison Fellowship (who also became a chaplain) say we were not chaplains at all. We were "secret subversives," he said. Yeah. Secret subversives. I liked that. Behind enemy lines.

I never made any pretense about my purpose for ministering on the inside. I was there to evangelize and disciple, pure and simple. I was a renegade chaplain ministering to redneck inmates. It was a great fit.

My ministry was spread out between five different prisons, all in the same county. Soon the state figured out it would be better for everyone if I could minister at just one location. That would be the Arrowhead Correctional Center.

On the exact day I was assigned to Arrowhead, Mike was transferred from a medium-security facility to Arrowhead. Neither of us knew about the other. How's that for providence?

The nickname for the Arrowhead prison was "Camp Snoopy." That's because the cons thought it was "easy time." The reality, however, was that while the place did not have the physical and forceful nature of a higher-security joint, Camp Snoopy messed with your head. That was something guys weren't used to. It just appeared to be easy time.

It was a joint where the cons got conned by the system. There was a lot of hostility and anxiety at Camp Snoopy. It was like a bad smell that wouldn't go away.

But many of the Christian convicts had the aroma of Christ. Spiritually speaking, they were lights in a dark place.

After Mike got settled at Camp Snoopy, he joined my ministry and became part of the chapel worship team. We witnessed God convict and convert hundreds of men. During my time at Camp Snoopy, over three hundred inmates were baptized.

While a chaplain I was in seminary too. School by day. Prison by night. Unlike the inmates, though, I got to go home at the end of the day. I had gotten caught up in the day-to-day work of ministry, racing here and there. I was attending seminary, raising financial support, raising a family, teaching inmates. Life became a fog. Eventually that fog got the best of me.

I couldn't recognize God's Kingdom through the razor wire, theology books, and family.

From a secular point of view, Camp Snoopy was a hostile work environment. From a spiritual point of view, it was one battle after another. I guess the guards were out to get me because I came across like I was on a crusade. My inexperience as a chaplain and my spiritual arrogance didn't help.

Being unaware of spiritual battles complicated things too.

But after getting my soul kicked around for a few years, I got humbled. In the process, I learned a simple and valuable lesson. Want respect? Then give respect. Eventually, I earned the respect of the guards.

It's amazing what a little humility and common sense can do for a person.

Looking back, I see that getting kicked around was linked to the deep spiritual battles. Connected for His purposes.

The battle has a cumulative effect. The battle humbled me. It shaped my understanding of God and how He connects the dots.

God was using me. Not that I ever doubted that. But I was missing some things. The enemy was using the guards to stop me. Harass me. Yet God used the sabotage of the guards to add fuel to the fire of His gospel. The very fire the guards were trying to put out. Only God!

God can take the crooked things men do and turn them around for good. For me, it took years for this lesson to sink in.

In fact, this is a gospel lesson. The cross, where men committed injustice against Jesus, was a crime scene. They murdered an innocent man. But what was meant for evil, God used for good. The murder of His Son was my redemption.

When rough stuff happened to me, like sabotage and the guards' betrayal, I got glimpses of what happened to Jesus. The more I embraced this kind of spiritual reality, through the lens of Jesus and His gospel, the more my life and ministry stayed on track.

Because my ministry was sabotaged so often, the results I experienced were amazing. That's how it works in the Kingdom. Just like the gospel. Upside down and inside out.

The Bible is a book about ongoing battles. Where there is opposition to the Lord, He shows Himself. Not only do spiritual battlegrounds make for good, fruit-producing fields, they are also good lesson fields for knuckleheads (like yours truly).

In the midst of this season, God began to use real life to teach me about His Kingdom. He used the most unlikely person: a convict.

One day, while I was walking across the prison yard, I saw Chuck, an inmate who was a good student and attended all my chapels and classes. He stopped and asked me a question that would change my life. "Hey, Chappy, what is the Kingdom of God?"

This was the last thing I would have expected him to ask, and it was a great spiritual question. However, I had no clue how to answer it. So I faked it. I said something theological, trying to hide my ignorance. I was embarrassed because I didn't know how to answer.

Good grief, I didn't even know the Kingdom of God was disguised as Camp Snoopy.

Chuck's question led me to a lifelong search for the answer. The question also inspired this book. More important, God used that question to grow His Kingdom and to teach others about it. A simple question from a faithful convict helped to connect the dots between my faith and God's Kingdom—and beyond.

This question became the rudder that would steer the course of my life.

I went back to a seminary prof and asked him about the Kingdom. No help there. It was like asking a chemist how love works.

There is great value in asking spiritual questions. I found out I just have to keep on asking.

It took me years to figure out how the Kingdom of God works. How to teach about it. How to experience it daily.

Yet here I was, immersed in conversions, making disciples, leading all kinds of good ministries to inmates and their families, but almost totally blind to His Kingdom. I couldn't define it or explain it, much less teach about it. I had to fake my answer to an inmate who truly wanted to know.

Being spiritually self-aware—both personally and concerning the Kingdom—has not been my strong suit. I could not use the excuse that I was surrounded by knucklehead cons. The "Aha!" answer about the Kingdom came many years later in Haiti, the location of my current ministry.

Still, I pressed on, blind to the Kingdom yet immersed in it at the same time. Living in it now. Waiting to see it realized in Heaven.

It's easy now to look back at Camp Snoopy and see the Kingdom. In fact, I now see it with 20/20 vision. I remember some amazing displays.

It was Christmastime, the one time of year when the guards gave the inmates more latitude for religious events. So I scheduled a Christmas Convict Caroling Crusade.

Camp Snoopy was set up in an oval, with five housing units forming the perimeter of the camp. The control center stood in the middle. An oval track and a prison yard sat between the housing units and the control center.

Every prison yard is a spiritual battlefield.

The Sunday before our Christmas Convict Caroling Crusade, I put out a sign-up sheet for the inmates. I wanted to see who had enough guts to parade around the track, singing and shouting about Jesus. Talk about proclaiming your weakness for all to see! More than fifty men signed up.

The day of the caroling was cold and overcast. Gray, breezy, and biting, with a miserable drizzle. Inmates trickled in, and I figured they were nervous, since many were late. Parading your faith around cops and fellow convicts is not easy. They can be a merciless crowd.

It took courage to walk onto that battlefield that day.

Maybe the gloomy weather had discouraged the men from coming out. I commend those cons for having the heart to sing about Jesus in such a hostile place in such lousy weather. The guards and the staff constantly teased the cons about being religious. Accountability in prison can be brutal.

Mike was the first one there, eager to lead. We handed out hymnals and started walking the track, singing the standard Christmas songs. After the first lap, the rest of the inmates who had signed up got the nerve to join in. Because of the weather, no inmates had come out to the yard.

As we marched around the track, our confidence grew. Mike and I led the way.

It was glorious. As we walked and sang, inmates watched us from almost every cell window, their noses against the glass and their hands cupped beside their faces to help them see. All the officers in the control center watched too. They were amazed.

Our faces were frozen, but we didn't care. After the traditional Christmas carols from the hymnal, we started belting out some of the Christian prison songs we sang in chapel every Sunday. Songs like "Pass Me Not," "Just a Closer Walk," and "One Day at a Time." We didn't need hymnals for these. We sang these songs so often, we all had them memorized. Then we started chanting like a Marine Corps unit. Coming up with our own lyrics as we sang. Just like we did in Sunday chapel. Mike and I belted out the lead lines, and the rest of the Christmas Convict Caroling Crusade responded with the echo:

*Hail Jesus you're my King (echo)*
*Your grace makes my heart sing (echo)*
*I will love you all my days (echo)*
*Perfect in all Your ways (echo)*
*Glory, glory to the Lamb (echo)*

You are the Promised Land (echo)

As we barked out this powerful, I-sing-it-you-sing-it song, wouldn't you know that it started to snow? God has a flair for the dramatic.

When I look back at Mike and me and all those cons singing around that track, all through the eyes of Jesus, it dawned on me what was going on: the Kingdom. I was demonstrating on the outside what was on the inside.

I was starting to get a handle on the Kingdom.

I finished my gig at Camp Snoopy a few years later. Mike did another ten years.

After that he was "off paper." A citizen. No parole. He had served every day of his time.

Inmates face intense temptation on release day. Those first twenty-four hours generally determine the path they walk for years ahead. (Wait till you hear about Jose). Mike was confused and alone. He had arrangements to stay at a shelter in Denver, but they had fallen through.

Our family had moved from Colorado back to Iowa. I remember being in some podunk Walmart when Mike called me from downtown Denver and asked what he should he do and where he should go.

God's sovereignty was running rampant that day in Walmart. During my years as a chaplain, I had ministered with a husband-and-wife team that helped released convicts transition back into society. I had not spoken to them about Mike for months, but they agreed to take him in.

I called Mike back and told him about his new home. God once again rescued my friend. His first rescue was salvation. Second was his prison cell. His third was when that couple accepted him into their home.

Over time, Mike became a key member of their ministry team. For ten years now, Mike has had the same full-time job since his release: helping released convicts transition back into the world.

Jesus said His Kingdom is like a mustard tree. Who would have guessed that its roots and branches can grow out of a prison yard? God certainly has some creative ways to connect the dots.

## *Connecting the Dots*

Arrowhead Correctional Center presents a bird's-eye view of the Kingdom. And as you zero in, you start to get a picture of the working parts.

- Repentance is always a great place to begin. And begin again, and again. The first words of Jesus when He began His ministry ...
- Repent! For the Kingdom of God is near! (Matthew 4:17)

- Not every con is a con. Just like not every churchgoer is for real. Christianity is not about playing spiritual games with God or others. It is for folks who are honest with God and honest with themselves before God.

- See what this godly sorrow [repentant attitude] has produced in you: what earnestness, what eagerness to clear yourselves, what indignation, what alarm, what longing, what concern, what readiness to see justice done. (2 Corinthians 7:11 NIV)

- My sacrifice, O God, is a broken spirit; a broken and contrite heart you, God, will not despise. (Psalm 51:17 NIV)

- "For this is what the high and exalted One says—he who lives forever, whose name is holy: 'I live in a high and holy place, but also with the one who is contrite and lowly in spirit, to revive the spirit of the lowly and to revive the heart of the contrite.'" (Isaiah 57:15 NIV)

- Real conviction of sin bears spiritual fruit, even from a prison cell. There is no substitute for genuine repentance. Mike's life is evidence of real repentance that led to an increase in the Kingdom of God. Look for a moment at Mike's life. Sixteen years doing time. Ministering on the inside. Getting out, then bearing fruit on the outside. Now consider this verse spoken by John the Baptist ...
  - "Bear fruit in keeping with repentance." (Matthew 3:8 ESV)
  - Ongoing repentance is key.

- I was so close to the Kingdom, yet I could not see it. Ironically, the things that caused my anxiety and stress were the signs showing I was immersed in it. For in these Kingdom battles, His mercy and grace and truth shine on a dark backdrop.
  - "Through many tribulations we must enter the Kingdom of God." (Acts 14:22 ESV)

- The Kingdom of God in which I was deeply immersed was also a sanctuary. That is why the inmates flooded to chapel and studies. They ran to the cross. They made nests in God's tree.
  - [Jesus] said therefore, "What is the Kingdom of God like? And to what shall I compare it? It is like a grain of mustard seed that a man took and sowed in his garden, and it grew and became a tree, and the birds of the air made nests in its branches" (Luke 13:18-19 ESV)

When that inmate asked me what the Kingdom of God is, I should have answered, "Camp Snoopy." I would have been spot on.

# Chapter 4
# Guilt on the Rocks

Jack was doing a life sentence for murder. No chance for parole.

As a Native American, Jack was a frequent visitor to the sweat lodge. The one at the prison was like any other Native American sweat lodge: a crude hut-like structure for prayer and communing with the spirits.

You go there to cook rocks. Get them real hot. Then you'd sit around them and sweat. Sweating was their means of spiritual purification—an atonement ritual. It was the Native American spiritual and ceremonial means to bring out the best in a person.

Sounds easy. Too easy.

In fact, it sounds absolutely crazy to me. But so does this …

The belief that some Cosmic Jewish Zombie can cleanse you and make you live forever. If you symbolically eat His flesh and telepathically tell Him you accept Him as your Master, He can free your soul from an evil force that is present in all humanity. All because a man didn't carry out his responsibility to protect his rib-woman wife from a talking snake who conned her into eating from a magical tree. And if you trust this Cosmic Jewish Zombie, you'll never die. You'll get to be reconciled to God and live in Heaven with Him forever.

This comment was written by an atheist who was mocking Christianity. I found it online back in the 90s, in the comments section following an article discussing the subject of God as Creator. He's edgy all right. But he sure has a handle on Jesus, faith, sin, the fall, Satan, Genesis, and Heaven.

I think we sometimes forget just how fantastic the story of our faith must sound to people. Me? I like the plot of this script. Write me in!

But not everyone thinks that way. Prisoners, like folks on the outside, are suspicious of clergy. When a clergy guy brings a message, some people are wary. They are unclear about the potential effects of our outrageous belief system. But what do you expect from the gospel story? It's downright incredible.

Most are skeptical of it from the git-go.

Sometimes in prison I saw more than just skepticism about Christianity. There is open hostility. Sometimes people so loathe Christian arrogance, Christian humility, or the Christian message that they return fire.

Other people hide behind the cross.

Jack thought he could hide his guilt under the rocks in the sweat lodge. He was a living example of a man who desperately needed atonement.

Jack taught me that a person can hide behind any belief system.

I was shocked, intrigued, encouraged, but not suspicious when Jack showed up at chapel service one Sunday. After an inmate visited chapel for the first time, I always went to his house. That's what inmates call their cells.

When I visited Jack, I had no idea he was in for an infamous murder. He had celebrity status on the inside. After I learned this, I became even more hopeful. It was exciting that a famous outlaw was on his way to faith in Jesus. I'll admit I got a little caught up in the spiritual glamour.

He kept coming to chapel. And after about two months, I started to have some regular spiritual talks with him. Jack was engaging and articulate.

Over time, he became quite real with his emotions. He even spoke to me of his crime. I checked his "blue sheet" (record and assessment). By golly, he was telling me the truth about his crime. The correctional officers (COs) were shocked by his openness with me. That's because he was known as a loner.

I scheduled a time to see Jack Saturday afternoon.

Saturday afternoons in the prison yard had a different feel from the rest of the week. It felt less like prison and more like a bunch of really bad dudes just hanging out. Mostly getting along.

It was an hour drive to the prison, and I prayed the entire way. Praying for Jack as I passed the razor wire. Praying as I walked across the prison yard. Jack's house was on the second floor of his housing unit. He had a room with a view, if you call the prison yard a view.

Our conversation turned spiritual. Now, after dozens of conversations and months of personal attention, we were praying and kneeling together before God in Jack's cell. I couldn't believe what was happening. I was caught up in the moment. He repeated a prayer I said, in which he confessed his sins, received forgiveness, and put his faith in Jesus.

The feeling in his cell was like the feeling in the prison yard on Saturday afternoons. Twilight zone.

Here we were. Two dudes making a connection with God.

Jack attended chapel the next two weeks. I went around telling all the guards of his amazing conversion. I was thrilled!

I was gamed. I was suckered. I was royally conned.

For months after Jack gamed me, the guards called me Chaplain Chocolate Heart. They enjoyed humiliating me over his fake conversion. It didn't work, not entirely. Lots of things in ministry can get under my skin. This episode didn't. Not too much, anyway. Still, things like that add up on a guy.

At the time I believed his conversion was real. It never occurred to me I was being set up.

I *was* a chocolate heart. That was a much-needed wake-up call.

But why did Jack do it? He never let me speak with him after his fake confession. In fact, he never made eye contact with me again, much less acknowledge my existence.

Jack went back to the sweat lodge. I will never understand how those rocks helped to cover his guilt. To purify him.

Don't your beliefs affect how you live your life? Common sense answers, "Of course!"

Did Jack mess with me only out of boredom? Was he under the influence of the enemy to harass me?

I was operating in the spiritual realm. Was Jack? Why set up a con game for three months to publicly humiliate someone?

If anything, it all points to the emptiness of how he

exercised his so-called faith.

What happens to a man's soul after he does something like that? Does his soul get so frosted that eventually he will die in his sin?

Here is what I think about Jack. I think he believes that Camp Snoopy is his kingdom. And when you have most of the guards and inmates laugh with you after your successful months-long con game, why wouldn't you think Camp Snoopy was your kingdom? That was Jack's domain.

Jack is currently on a collision course. Sweating out atonement for purification was not going to work. His only remedy was the gospel. And yet that gospel, that Kingdom, was freely offered to him. Both publicly and personally. Like the quote from the atheist, he was filled with contempt and scorn for Christianity.

Men will always be responsible to answer to their Creator. That's why all the smack the guards talked about me never bothered me much.

All that gaming was Jack's loss, not mine. I have never taken the credit for the conversion of a soul. A soul is not mine to win. For that matter, it's not mine to lose, either. That's up to God.

The Holy Spirit is the Convicter of sin. To be convicted sounds bad. From the courts? Maybe. From God? Definitely not. Being convicted by the Holy Spirit? That's something we all need.

I provided some good entertainment for Jack for a couple of months. He sought to amuse himself at the expense of God's Spirit and grace. I'm sure he thought I was better entertainment than MeTV.

I learned some valuable lessons from that spiritual battle.

Whether you're in a church or a prison cell, repeating religious words that aren't from the heart is meaningless. Or worse. It has the opposite effect of purification: it distances the soul from God. I'm certain God wants to hear from the heart, not from a parrot. That's just spiritual common sense.

Never again in my evangelism did I ever do the "I say it and then you say it" prayer.

If you are going to fight for the souls of men, then you had better discern there are powers intentionally coming against you, and your King, and His Kingdom.

Deception and humiliation—these are standard weapons from the enemy's arsenal. Satan himself loads the guns.

He's been intentionally sabotaging the Kingdom of God since creation.

Every kingdom has a king. Jack wanted to rule his kingdom. I want to rule mine. You want to rule yours.

To understand the Kingdom of God is to humble ourselves and be honest before God. To find purification in His sovereign truth. No matter how crazy that may seem.

## *Connecting the Dots*

- The only sweat that points to our salvation was the sweat poured out by Jesus in the garden before He died.

- And being in anguish, he prayed more earnestly, and his sweat was like drops of blood falling to the ground. (Luke 22:44 NIV)

- While our faith in God is expressed with wisdom and common sense, it's clear that God's ways are mysterious.

- Do you not know? Have you not heard? The Lord is the everlasting God, the Creator of the ends of the earth. He will not grow tired or weary, and his understanding no one can fathom. (Isaiah 40:28 NIV)

- "He performs wonders that cannot be fathomed, miracles that cannot be counted." (Job 5:9 NIV)

- Oh, the depth of the riches of the wisdom and knowledge of God! How unsearchable his judgments, and his paths beyond tracing out! (Romans 11:33 NIV)

- For the message of the cross is foolishness to those who are perishing, but to us who are being saved it is the power of God. (1 Corinthians 1:18 NIV)

- Jack was in chapel for months and visited with me for hours. Why won't people believe? Why does one believe and another does not? The Bible tells us why.

- The person without the Spirit does not accept the

things that come from the Spirit of God but considers them foolishness, and cannot understand them because they are discerned only through the Spirit. (1 Corinthians 2:14 NIV)

- "A person can receive only what is given them from Heaven." (John 3:27 NIV)

- "And this is the judgment: the light has come into the world, and people loved the darkness rather than the light because their works were evil. For everyone who does wicked things hates the light and does not come to the light, lest his works should be exposed." (John 3:19-20 ESV)

- For the mind that is set on the flesh is hostile to God, for it does not submit to God's law; indeed, it cannot. (Romans 8:7 ESV)

- What does God want? He wants many things. A good place to start is humility.

- "He has shown you, O mortal, what is good. And what does the Lord require of you? To act justly and to love mercy and to walk humbly with your God." (Micah 6:8 NIV)

- Do nothing out of selfish ambition or vain conceit, but in humility consider others better than yourselves. Each of you should look not only to your own interests, but also to the interest of others. Your attitude should be the same as that of Christ Jesus. (Philippians 2:3-5)

- The enemy moves with stealth in the Kingdom of God.

- Jesus told them another parable: "The Kingdom of Heaven is like a man who sowed good seed in his field. But while everyone was sleeping, his enemy came and sowed weeds among the wheat, and went away. When the wheat sprouted and formed heads, then the weeds also appeared." (Matthew 13:24-26 NIV)

- Be alert and of sober mind. Your enemy the devil prowls around like a roaring lion looking for someone to devour. Resist him, standing firm in the faith. (1 Peter 5:8-9 NIV)


- Only God and God alone—not a convict, not a chaplain—is sovereign over every Kingdom. God reigns. And His reign is perfect in every way.

- For in him [Jesus] all things were created: things in Heaven and on earth, visible and invisible, whether thrones or powers or rulers or authorities; all things have been created through him and for him. He is before all things, and in him all things hold together. (Colossians 1:16-17 NIV)

- For from him and through him and for him are all things. To him be the glory forever! Amen. (Romans 11:36 NIV)

God knows nothing of the unexpected.

# Chapter 5
# Criminal Thinking Error #8

A voice echoed off the walls in the prison yard. "Hey, Chaplain! Jose told me to tell you he didn't mean to shoot that cop!"

This next story borders on the ridiculous … (pondering)… Scratch that. Borders are crossed. It *is* ridiculous.

Jose hounded me for months to baptize him before he got released from prison. I tried to explain to him that being convicted of a crime is not the same as being convicted of your sins. He had a hard time with this. Jose was Knucklehead First Class.

Living in prison is like living in a fishbowl. If the inmates didn't know your business, the cops did. Everyone loved telling the chaplain who was messing up.

When Jose pleaded his case for baptism, I was skeptical. I knew the line on Jose. Even just a brief listen to Jose told me where he was coming from.

After every Sunday evening chapel service, Jose was the first guy asking to be baptized. "Okay, Jose. I'll keep an eye on you. I'll stop by your cell this week, and we'll talk."

Jose's cell was literally a pornographic mural. Two walls and half the ceiling were pinup whores. I asked him why he wanted to be baptized. He said he had a chance to sell his porn collection, so it was a good time to get baptized.

Now you know why I included knuckleheads in the

title of this book.

When I talked to Jose about God's Spirit, about being spiritually reborn, his eyes glazed over the same way mine did in seventh-grade algebra.

Guards, counselors, and parole officers are always all over convicts about being "religious." Religiosity is the behavior that says to the world, "Now that I have religion, I'm good."

On the prison radar screen, that is called CTE #8: Religiosity.

CTE stands for Criminal Thinking Error. A list of all the CTEs was published for everyone in the substance abuse and sex offender programs at Camp Snoopy. And if there was ever a textbook case of CTE #8, it was Jose.

Jose wasn't into spiritual things. He wanted to be, sort of. He just couldn't connect the dots. What he lacked spiritually, he made up for in prison transactions. He said his roomie could make some money by renting all the porn he had taken off his walls.

Even after a little pastoral counsel, Jose still had a difficult time understanding what taking down the pornography from his walls had to do with following Jesus.

On our way to the ridiculous, we find Jose crossing line after line.

Why was he dull to these things? Was it a matter of intelligence? No. I don't think so. Well ... maybe (JK). It was a matter of the heart, not the brain. Of motivation. God will never turn away anyone who genuinely seeks Him. Jose was in it for personal gain. And to make himself look good.

I returned to Jose's crib a week later and encountered no porn. Yet I was still skeptical. "Hey, Jose, what did you do with all that porn?"

"I sold it to my roomie. But I ain't got no more porn, Chappy! Can I be baptized now?"

You have to work really hard to get into prison. I'm not kidding. The system is designed that way. Only knuckleheads with a capital "N" make it in. Along the way, guys usually pick up some small doses of humility. Maybe a little understanding. Not Jose.

When he saw I wasn't buying his "I'm a Christian now" story, he started having his buddies try to convince me that he was a new man. This went on for about a month. He and his pals really worked me. I did see some changes in Jose for a while. And against my better judgment, I baptized Jose the Sunday before he was released.

A week later, when his buddy tried to encourage me from across the prison yard, I already knew about Jose's latest crime. I had read about it on the front page of the Rocky Mountain News.

That Chaplain! Another chocolate heart episode. Sucker. Those words never got to me too much. It was my hope to see convicts convicted of their sin. Because I wanted this so much, I got suckered. But then again, everyone gets gamed in prison. No one is immune.

With Jose, there was no sorrow. No sense of his sin. Or anybody else's sin, for that matter.

When God convicts people of their sin, His Spirit, the Holy Spirit, is working inside them. But Jose never attempted to seek Him, or even begin to rely on God's Spirit.

This just makes a prison sentence that much longer. It's sad that people like doing time. Like Jose, they get used to prison. And after a while, they see nothing wrong with their hearts, surrounded by smutty walls in dimly lit rooms.

Jose has a great opportunity for God to show him the power of His Spirit. For God is the God of second chances. Third, fourth, fifth, and on and on.

As for now, Jose is in just the right place for those extra chances. A cozy private room in maximum security 23/7 lockdown (an hour a day for exercise and hygiene).

There is still hope for Jose. That's because there is no place on earth where God's Spirit cannot reach. Even beyond the ridiculous.

## *Connecting the dots ...*

- Jose knew baptism held a special meaning. It is a very spiritual thing. But it's not going to take you across the salvation bridge. Only the blood of Christ, applied by His Spirit, will do that.

- Jesus answered, 'Truly, truly, I say to you, unless one is born of water and the Spirit, he cannot enter the Kingdom of God." (John 3:5 ESV)

- "I will give you a new heart and put a new spirit in you; I will remove from you your heart of stone and give you a heart of flesh. And I will put my Spirit in you and move you to follow my decrees and be careful to keep my laws. Then you will live in the land I gave your ancestors; you will be my people, and I will be your God. I will save you from all your uncleanness." (Ezekiel 36:26-29 NIV)

- He saved us, not because of righteous things we had done, but because of his mercy. He saved us through the washing of rebirth and renewal by the Holy Spirit, whom he poured out on us generously through Jesus Christ our Savior. (Titus 3:5-6 NIV)

- The Holy Spirit and Jesus are our eternal security. God cannot break a promise He made. He not only promises our guarantee through His Spirit, but He is the Guarantor as well. That's a capital G!

- When you believed, you were marked in him with a seal, the promised Holy Spirit, who is a deposit guaranteeing our inheritance until the redemption of

- those who are God's possession—to the praise of his glory. (Ephesians 1:13-14 NIV)
- Because of this oath, Jesus has become the guarantor of a better covenant. (Hebrews 7:22 NIV)

- Jose was trying to prove to me his righteousness. No person's righteousness could ever be sufficient to satisfy God. Jose equated being spiritual with a ceremony. Sorry, buddy. Only the righteousness of Jesus will do. We get His righteousness as a gift when we receive Him by faith.
- Not having a righteousness of my own that comes from the law, but that which is through faith in Christ—the righteousness that comes from God on the basis of faith. (Philippians 3:9 NIV)
- God made him who had no sin to be sin for us, so that in him we might become the righteousness of God. (2 Corinthians 5:21 NIV)

- Hypocrisy and playing spiritual games are signs of being deceived.
- This is the message we have heard from him and declare to you: God is light; in him there is no darkness at all. If we claim to have fellowship with him and yet walk in the darkness, we lie and do not live out the truth. But if we walk in the light, as he is in the light, we have fellowship with one another, and the blood of Jesus, his Son, purifies us from all sin. If we claim to be without sin, we deceive ourselves and the

truth is not in us. If we confess our sins, he is faithful and just and will forgive us our sins and purify us from all unrighteousness. If we claim we have not sinned, we make him out to be a liar and his word is not in us. (1 John 1:5-10 NIV)

- Before we are quick to judge Jose, we had better take a good look at ourselves.
- "Why do you look at the speck of sawdust in your brother's eye and pay no attention to the plank in your own eye? How can you say to your brother, 'Let me take the speck out of your eye,' when all the time there is a plank in your own eye? You hypocrite, first take the plank out of your own eye, and then you will see clearly to remove the speck from your brother's eye." (Matthew 7:3-5 NIV)

- Being in a position of spiritual authority requires discernment.
- "Do not give dogs what is sacred; do not throw your pearls to pigs. If you do, they may trample them under their feet, and turn and tear you to pieces." (Matthew 7:6 NIV)

- What does God want? Yes, He wants to be obeyed. But not just for the sake of obedience. It's a matter of love and faith. What else does God want? From Jose? From you and me? He wants to be believed. And from genuine faith in Him flows obedient devotion.

- "Not everyone who says to me, 'Lord, Lord,' will enter the Kingdom of Heaven, but only the one who does the will of my Father who is in Heaven. Many will say to me on that day, 'Lord, Lord, did we not prophesy in your name and in your name drive out demons and in your name perform many miracles?' Then I will tell them plainly, 'I never knew you. Away from me, you evildoers!'" (Matthew 7:21-23 NIV)

It was obvious what Jose was missing in his pursuit of righteousness. What's in *your* wallet?

# Chapter 6
# Job is Not a Republican

They say a year in prison ministry is like ten in the pastorate. So I did, like, a hundred dog years of prison ministry.

When I left Camp Snoopy, I was fried to a delicate crunch. Burned out—pronounced: Burnt. Out.

Prison is full of knuckleheads and bullies. I found the ratio of bully cops to bully inmates to be pretty even. After I battled with bullies for almost ten years in prison ministry, the bullies almost got the best of me.

Near the end of my chaplaincy, I drove down the mountain one Sunday and pulled into the parking lot at the prison. I sat in my car and wept. I couldn't get out of the car. I couldn't preach one more sermon. The well was dry. My soul was spent. I found a guard who was going on duty and asked him to tell my inmate "church" that I was sick and wouldn't be there that day.

I stayed home that day and the next, trying to regain my composure. A few months later, I finished my time at Camp Snoopy.

I decided to take a year off to find out whether I should even be in ministry anymore.

After a year of soul searching, I ended up in a small church in rural Iowa. I counted on the ratio of bullies to ministers being more in my favor out here in Iowa. Looking back, I realize that thought is laughable. Cornfields make for great hideouts.

I was naïve to think I could find a bully-free zone anywhere.

I admire a man who can, with grace and dignity, stand up to a bully. A man who can wholeheartedly listen to an entirely jacked-up point of view from a bully and then keep on smiling. That was Larry. Larry wasn't a Christian when we met. Yet he taught me valuable lessons about grace and bullies.

Larry lived across the road from the little country church most of his life. A well-liked fellow in the community, he was soft spoken. Gentle. Caring. As a teenager, Larry lost a leg in an accident, but that didn't alter his positive outlook. He was a very successful businessman with a beautiful family of three daughters and a loving and supportive wife. Larry also had terminal cancer when we met. He was nearing the end of his life.

During my first week as pastor, Larry came over to my office and introduced himself. I immediately liked him. He asked if his family could use the church building for his daughter's wedding. Of course! As pastor, I was also chief cook and bottle washer. That meant I had a part in setting things up for the ceremony. That's when our friendship began.

Whenever I spoke with Larry, he made me feel like the most important person in the room. That's a special gift.

After the wedding, I asked Larry to join us for our weekly men's Bible study. He kindly explained that he did not share my view of Christianity. He believed everyone went to Heaven, regardless of what they believed. He said Jesus was a good man but not necessary to get to Heaven. Larry never believed Jesus was God. Or the Savior.

Larry's biggest hurdle to overcome was reconciling

the God of the Old Testament with Jesus.

He couldn't get past the anger of God in the Old Testament. The Jesus he knew could never match the "angry" God of the Old Testament.

Then he called and graciously agreed to attend Bible study. At the time, I was unaware of his illness.

I was pleased that Larry attended. But it sure bugged Hal. Hal was the church know-it-all. A bully. He could get under your skin faster than engine grease. Hal's primary mission in life was to argue with anyone who didn't agree with him. His second priority was to recruit you into the Republican party.

At our first Bible study as the new pastor, I'd assumed I would teach. But Hal bullied his way in. All the guys from church were there, including Larry. Hal knew what Larry believed. And it wasn't anywhere close to anything he had to say. Not just about theology, but politics too. Not only that, but Hal's manner of speaking and the aggressive ways he went about things made him hard to be around.

I'm three-quarters redneck and don't go in for all that Kumbaya jazz. Hal got us guys to stand in a circle and hold hands to pray. I got real uncomfortable real fast. Especially with Larry there.

After I wiped the sweat off my hands, Hal updated us with the latest news of the Republican National Committee. After a few weeks of Hal, I was ready to vote for anyone with a 'D' next to their name.

I don't remember what we studied. But whatever it was, Hal made sure we knew all his answers. The biggest impression those Bible studies left on me was not that

Hal was a big jerk, but that Larry was patient, kind, and gracious to everyone there. He was a good example for me. He rarely agreed with anything Hal said. Larry didn't say much of anything at these studies.

The political stuff went on side by side with the Bible studies for months. Larry was there almost every week. I could hardly believe he continued to show up. By example, Larry was the best teacher at our study.

After about six months, Larry told me about his cancer. He never looked sick. But he was. Larry was very private. He was one of the most honest people I have ever met. Which made for an honest friendship between us.

I wanted to be an encouragement to Larry. We both loved breakfast food and we enjoyed going out for biscuits and gravy or eggs and pancakes. Redneck chow.

But as his illness progressed, Larry's appetite and energy faded, and our get-togethers moved from the diner to his living room. We talked there frequently. Larry had the best stories. As time went on, our visits got shorter. He never wanted me to see him taken by his cancer, and I respected that.

We often talked about our views of God. As the weeks went on, Larry knew I was evangelizing him. If he could put up with Hal, certainly Larry could put up with me. And he did. I did my best to be gentle, since our beliefs were vastly different.

Essentially, Larry and I argued about theology. About salvation. Only we were soft spoken and respectful to one another. Actually, I do not think Larry was arguing so much with me as he was with God.

As nice as Larry was in disagreeing with me, he wanted his salvation to coincide with his theology. He wanted salvation on his terms. He knew he was at odds with the Bible.

People will always find an angle to argue with the good news of God's grace.

Larry had a soft view of sin. When I spoke about God being angry at sin, even hating it, I could almost see him cringe. When I asked Larry what God does with truly "bad" people, he didn't have an answer.

We had dozens of discussions on the many ways God expresses His grace. We talked about how the Old Testament compares with the New Testament. This was tough for Larry. So was reconciling God and suffering. He listened patiently. He was inquisitive.

Yet as our conversations ended, he would politely say he just didn't need the grace of Jesus. He figured everybody already had salvation, and faith in God wasn't necessary.

Larry was respectfully stubborn.

Regardless of our theological differences, we were pals. As a friend, I never wanted to see Larry suffer.

Larry identified with Job. He had not lost his wealth, but like Job, Larry was losing his health and his life. He often asked me about Job.

At that specific time, I had not come to fully understand the book of Job. But I wasn't completely clueless. My problem was that I never understood the "why" of Job. Why did he suffer? Why all the mystery surrounding his losses? Why the lousy friends? What "reasoning" do we walk away with after we read Job?

What was God saying through Job?

Years later, in my own season of suffering, I learned that God was pointing to Christ through Job. Job was a figure of Christ. Knowing that would change the way I would endure suffering. If Job and Jesus transcended suffering as a means to glorify God, where does that leave me as a Christian? It clarifies suffering. Dignity, peace, and assurance can point to the power of God in me.

Suffering now has purpose. This made Jesus become very real, personal, and relatable. For me to see the humanity of Christ, the suffering and shame He took, and how that fit perfectly within the plan of God ... well, this realization overwhelmed me. In a good way. Now I saw a divine purpose that transcended suffering. If it happened with Job and Jesus, it can apply to me. Now in everything that happens, easy or difficult, I can give glory to God.

But when I was with Larry, I had not yet come to this understanding of Job. In this particular season, I too was like Larry. How do I reconcile the pain of suffering with the goodness of God? I needed to answer this question from the gut. From down deep. I needed clear answers. Short. To the point. I couldn't argue lofty arguments and be heard.

I figured the best way to get an answer on this subject was to read my Bible. So I read Job. Over and over. It was then God gave me a degree of understanding Job's suffering. I had to share this wonderful news with Larry.

That's when it happened. I went to visit Larry on a

beautiful spring day. I remember the trees were in bloom. He was sitting out on his front lawn under a huge shade tree with white blossoms. The weather was perfect. It was so still. He was there with his daughters and wife. I pulled up a chair and joined them.

We chatted for a while. That strange awkward feeling of death was inescapable. Yet the moment was still enjoyable. When the time was right, I asked if I could tell him about a sweet understanding I had just learned from reading Job. Larry was his usual kind self and said with a smile, "Of course."

No one was more broken than Job. Many people can relate to some of Job's losses. Losing a child. A business. Your health. But all of these? All at the same time? And then the "friends" that pile on? How do you speak to someone who has gone through such a total loss? It doesn't take a rocket scientist to figure out you don't use guilt. And you certainly don't scream at them.

The words at the very end of Job held the insight. God had questions for Job in the midst of his suffering. "Were you there when I laid the earth's foundation?" "Have you journeyed to the springs of the sea or walked in the recesses of the deep?" The unanswerable questions from God went on and on, chapter after chapter. All in the form of poetry. Beautiful, tender poetry. And then in the midst of those soft words came God's ultimate question for Job. "Would you condemn me to justify yourself?"

I asked Larry, "How do you think these questions would sound coming from the voice of God to an utterly broken man? What tone of voice do you imagine God would use to a man who had lost everything?"

The key to unlocking God's tone of voice would be found in Job's response.

Job's response to God's questioning was humility, and peace, and repentance.

Had God used a harsh or scolding tone with Job, given Job's deeply bruised emotional state, it would have crushed him. We saw that by the way Job's friends spoke to him. But God, the God of the Old Testament, who is the Jesus of the New, was not harsh in tone or temperament with Job in his questioning. Just the opposite. He was gentle. And with each passing question, in the tenderness of God's voice, Job and Larry would hear the compassion of God.

At that moment Larry broke. Almost like Job. Right in front of his wife and daughter, Larry began to shed a few tears. Then he confessed Christ. It was powerful. It was something his family had been waiting for and praying for. Larry wept. Then he laughed. He cried some more and then he laughed some more. His conversion was amazingly gentle. Just like God.

Three days later, Larry passed. The funeral was huge. Hundreds of people gathered at a large church in a nearby town. Larry surprised me. He had his wife ask me to co-officiate his funeral with another pastor. That was like a parting gift from Larry to me. I was able to proclaim God's sovereign grace. I shared Larry's testimony.

In those three days between his confession of Christ and his passing, Larry made a video. In it, he confessed his newfound faith. He graciously thanked me and his family pastor. His gratitude to God was on display at the funeral for all to see.

Larry was a funny guy too. At the end of the video, as everyone was being dismissed, he played the theme song from "The Benny Hill Show," the silly English comedian. That was Larry. Smiling till the end.

At the reception after the service, four different people sought me out and told me how each of them had shared the gospel with Larry at different points in his life. One described how she shared the gospel with him after he'd lost his leg in the accident. Another told me he shared Jesus when they were in college together. A former partner told Larry about the cross while they were in the insurance business together. After Larry's cancer diagnosis, another friend shared with him the hope found in the cross. I stood more and more amazed at God's wooing with each testimony.

Who knows how many "Hals" Larry had in his life? You know, the type of Christian who tends to put the unbeliever on the defensive. Who by their unloving demeanor provoke people to defend an unbiblical theology.

On the other hand, I believe that all those friends who planted the seeds of the gospel in Larry's soul had a cumulative effect. I believe their gospel words contributed to the moment when Larry rose above his personal theology of ungrace. Through Larry's friends, God had been wooing Larry his entire life.

Both Larry and Job argued with God for a long time. God won and then gave them both the ultimate prize.

The soft voice of God speaking to a dying man was sweet salvation for Larry.

Jesus was not so fortunate. He was the One chosen to be the Substitute.

On the cross, Jesus heard what a forgiven sinner will never hear: the harsh tone of a God who has no tolerance of sin. Because Jesus took upon Himself all the sins of all the sinners He came to die for, He heard the Father's words of scorn and condemnation of sin and sinners. This is why Jesus cried out, "My God, my God, why have you forsaken me?"

The only person who can appease God's anger toward sin is God Himself. That would be Jesus. God was satisfied with Jesus's sacrifice. Jesus stood in the path of God's wrath on Larry's behalf. This is grace.

Larry was blessed to know the sounds of grace, the mercy in God's voice, before it was too late.

## *Connecting the Dots*

Theology matters.

- Jesus is God. From before the creation of this world to this present day, God is consistent.
- "I the Lord do not change." (Malachi 3:6 NIV)
- Jesus Christ is the same yesterday today and forever. (Hebrews 13:8 NIV)
- "Very truly I tell you," Jesus answered, "before Abraham was born, I am!" (John 8:58 NIV)
- When God spoke to Moses from the burning bush, He used the exact same words as in the above passage: "I am!"

- Job knew about Jesus. I don't know how he knew. But it is clear that he did indeed know. The following verse from Job proves it and provides another link that proves the God of the Old Testament and the Jesus of the New Testament are one and the same.
- "For I know that my Redeemer lives, and at the last he will stand upon the earth. And after my skin has been thus destroyed, yet in my flesh I shall see God, whom I shall see for myself, and my eyes shall behold, and not another." (Job 19:25-27 ESV)

- Hal's approach was blunt and insensitive. When you fight for God's Kingdom, you don't use the weapons of the world. Fight like Jesus. With humility, patience, gentleness, and boldness. That's a tough balance. But it's the Christian call.

- But in your hearts revere Christ as Lord. Always be prepared to give an answer to everyone who asks you to give the reason for the hope that you have. But do this with gentleness and respect. (1 Peter 3:15 NIV)

- Therefore, as God's chosen people, holy and dearly loved, clothe yourselves with compassion, kindness, humility, gentleness and patience. (Colossians 3:12 NIV)

- Over the course of Larry's life, his friends planted seeds, the words of the Gospel, in Larry's soul. God allows us to be part of an increasing Kingdom, the salvation of souls.

- I planted the seed, Apollos watered it, but God has been making it grow. (1 Corinthians 3:6 NIV)

- "As the rain and the snow come down from Heaven, and do not return to it without watering the earth and making it bud and flourish, so that it yields seed for the sower and bread for the eater, so is my word that goes out from my mouth: It will not return to me empty, but will accomplish what I desire and achieve the purpose for which I sent it." (Isaiah 55:10-11 NIV)

- What Larry had trouble believing was that God does indeed get angry. Accepting anger as one of God's emotions is difficult for folks. He gets angry at sin. He hates it. But He is the only one who has what it takes to appease His own anger toward sin.

- For all have sinned and fall short of the glory of God,

and are justified by his grace as a gift, through the redemption that is in Christ Jesus, whom God put forward as a propitiation [satisfaction for God's wrath] by his blood, to be received by faith. (Romans 3:23-25 ESV)

- In this is love, not that we have loved God but that he loved us and sent his Son to be the propitiation [appeasement of God's wrath] for our sins. (1 John 4:10 ESV)


- Larry's theology said he could have salvation apart from Christ. This is a common error. When Larry "argued" with me, he was showing the spiritual struggle between what he believed about salvation versus what God said and did for him. All arguments aside, the only foundation for salvation is Jesus.

- Salvation is found in no one else, for there is no other name under Heaven given to mankind by which we must be saved. (Acts 4:12 NIV)

- Jesus answered, "I am the way and the truth and the life. No one comes to the Father except through me." (John 14:6 NIV)

I'm really happy for Larry that God settled this argument.

# Chapter 7
# A Deaf Man Hears from God

Benny was dying from brain cancer. And his wife, Dorothy, didn't seem to care.

The idea that God would forgive her husband made her angry. She wasn't shy about saying that either, even though she was a lifelong churchgoer. I don't know what he did earlier in their marriage, but he'd hurt her badly, and she didn't hide it.

Benny was Larry's neighbor. He lived right across the road. They both had cancer and died within weeks of one another. It was all so strange. At the time, I figured I was simply dealing with basic spiritual needs. Looking back, the timing and context seem supernatural.

Benny's spiritual house was all very confusing to me. I could help him, but there wasn't much I could do for Dorothy. Her heart was tired. Heavy. Hard. Distant. But Benny was open. He wanted to hear about Jesus.

I decided to do a quick assessment to see where he was, spiritually speaking.

Back when I was a prison chaplain, I had developed a method to discover an inmate's relationship to Jesus. It wasn't foolproof, but was it quick and helped me discern. I tried this same kind of questioning with Benny. Here is roughly how the conversation went.

"Hey, Benny, what was your mother's name?"

"Margaret."

"Who was your favorite uncle?"

"Uncle Joe."

"Who was your best pal in the fifth grade?"
"Johnny."
Then I reversed the process.
"Who is Margaret?"
"My mom."
"Who is Joe?"
"My favorite uncle."
"Who is Johnny?"
"My best pal in fifth grade."

And then, seemingly out of the blue, I asked this next question. A hard, over-the-top breaking curve ball.

"So, Benny, who's Jesus?"

A lot of people would be caught looking. Huh? Jesus?

If their answer didn't have the word "my" in it, I knew I had work to do.

If the answer was something like, "Jesus is God," the person knew something of the nature of Jesus. But if the word "my" was spoken in their answer, it demonstrated something personal about their relationship with God. If I heard "My Lord," or "My Savior," I saw a connection to Jesus. A bond.

When I asked Benny who Jesus was, he was honest. He said he didn't have a clue. Fair enough.

Benny was a hardcore sports fan. He loved his Iowa Hawkeyes. The NFL. The St. Louis Cardinals. Me too. I loved watching football with Benny. Even though he was borderline deaf and had to listen to the TV through his headphones. When you wanted to talk to him, you had to wave your arms to get his attention and then shout so he could hear you.

Since the church was right next door to his house, it

was easy for me to stop by. I'd come around back to the sliding door, open it, and scream, "Hey, Benny, mind if I come watch the game with you?" And then with a deaf man's voice he would yell back at me, "Ure, um ah ih." (Translated "Sure, come on in.")

I got to shout the gospel to him plenty of times. He heard it. This went on for about six months.

All this drove Dorothy crazy. She would roll her eyes. Suck her teeth. Fold her arms. She had to care for this deaf old codger who had made her early years miserable. Now this? No disrespect, but I found it somewhat amusing.

Still, Dorothy dogged him with guilt after I told him about Jesus.

After a while, it got to be sort of a game. He treated her badly all these years, and soon he would be leaving her. And she used his coming departure against him too. She was more than angry at him. She was bitter and filled with contempt. I could see that. I made sure that, when I yelled the gospel to him, I always screamed about forgiveness. I was communicating to Dorothy too, but I don't think she ever connected the dots.

Benny always smiled after I shouted the gospel to his deaf ears. He smiled and nodded a lot. And he communicated by looking directly into my eyes. He loved hearing about forgiveness and didn't seem to mind the constant reminders to repent of his sins. I guess I'd be hungry for forgiveness too if I were in his shoes.

One of the best things about ministering in this podunk community was the fishing hole I found. Go down the blacktop east of town. Turn right at the first gravel road. Then left at the next gravel road. Take a right where the fence opens to the field. Careful over the stream. Then up the steep bank.

This bass pond was surrounded by a variety of mature trees. I couldn't see a single house or road from there. This was my personal sanctuary. And the fish? Dang! Two-to-five pound large-mouth bass were common. Those big daddies would hit so hard on topwater lures, it made me laugh out loud. Smack. And watch them dance on their tails above the waterline. Hoo-wee! Redneck bass Heaven.

I told Benny about all the fun I was having at the pond. He reminisced about his good ol' days of bass fishing. But now Benny could hardly walk. I rigged up a comfy chair in my van for him and took him with me. We parked at the side of the pond on top of the manmade dam.

Benny was sitting inside, in his comfy chair, a big cheesy grin on his face. With the sliding door to the van all the way open, I threw out the line for him.

One of my biggest thrills was watching his face when a big bass hit his lure. "I ot wah! I ot wah!" he shouted (I got one! I got one!). It was like taking someone to see the Rocky Mountains for the first time. Or riding the roller coaster over and over again with your buddy. Off you go, riding and screaming together. This wasn't Benny's first bass. But it sure felt like the first time all over again, for Benny and for me.

I don't know exactly the day when Jesus applied His forgiveness to Benny's soul.

But this particular day, I shouted from the back door,

"Hey, Benny, it's Jeff. Can I come in? "Ure, may ore ell omfoble" (Sure, make yourself comfortable.) Dorothy wasn't home this day. More divine sovereignty running rampant. This helped because she had a tendency to cramp our style every time we were together. A real buzzkill.

This day, the timing belonged to God. As we shouted back and forth, the conversation turned to Benny's imminent death. And then I threw him that overhand curve ball. And bang! He homered. Big time!

This day, I asked him again, "Hey, Benny, who's Jesus?"

Benny said it. "Ee's my rend!" (He's my friend.)

From not having a clue to "my friend!" Now that's God!

Over the next few days, I talked to Benny about faith, forgiveness, and the Holy Spirit. And about baptism. About what it meant. I told him baptism was about showing God and others that he was serious about his new God-given faith. About the symbolism of washing his soul. About a new heart and Jesus making him clean. And that he was part of God's church now. He got it. No problem.

Then from his deaf man's voice he shouted two words I'll never forget. "Wah me!" (Wash me!)

Benny may have been deaf but he heard God.

I brought a few fellows from church with me that day to baptize Benny. I made sure one of them wasn't Hal. I didn't want any interference.

Benny sat in his overstuffed recliner in front of his TV. We put towels all around him, behind his back, on his shoulders, and on his lap. It probably would have hurt Benny to put him in the dunk tank and put his head below the water. So instead, I poured a large pitcher of water over his bald head. He loved it.

The sound of this deaf, dying man shouting out his confession of Jesus just before his baptism is forever burned on my brain. The memory of his voice, his confession of faith, will never leave me. This is what Benny cried out before I doused him. "I belee Eesus ih Gah. My Gah. My Avior. I belee ou, Eesus. Ank ou or orgiving me." (I believe Jesus is God. My God. My Savior. I believe You, Jesus. Thank You for forgiving me.)

After his baptism was over, he couldn't stop giving thanks. What an experience!

Benny acted like every truly forgiven man acts after he receives salvation—he worshipped.

This guy had never darkened the doors of a church his entire life. It took me thirty seconds to walk from Benny's back porch to the church building. In Benny's condition, it took him fifteen minutes. But he didn't mind. He liked using the headphones we had in the front pews so he could hear the service.

I knew his conversion was real. On many levels. One thing was especially striking. Benny wasn't in his overstuffed recliner waiting to watch the first game of the NFL doubleheader on Sundays. Nope. Benny was at worship.

After his conversion, Benny's wife got even angrier. Now she had to deal with God's grace toward someone she felt did not deserve it. She was right about that. Benny didn't deserve it. That's why it's called grace. She didn't deserve it either. Who does?

Benny didn't go to church to make her upset. He went there to thank God for his salvation. He was faithful until the end. Just a few months later, he passed.

It's sad because I don't think Dorothy ever believed her husband's conversion was real. She didn't want to. She could not stomach the thought that God would use His blood to forgive this man who had hurt her all those years. She confessed herself a Christian, but what she wanted for her husband was justice, not grace.

Imagine a murdered Christian woman running into her murderer in Heaven. That's how Dorothy saw all this.

I spoke to her every time I stopped by to see Benny and her. She put on a front and acted as if she had the whole "Christian thing" figured out. She never let me past her spiritual walls.

Jesus gave His life to pay God for my sins. Because death could not hold Him, it cannot hold me. This is the simple gospel message Benny clung to. The message that made him want to worship.

Someday, the three of us (Benny, me, and Jesus) will be off at some perfect pond hooking some more big daddies. There won't be any need for shouting. Ears and voices will work perfectly. No one will think about cancer. Ever. God will have taken care of our souls and our bodies.

Best of all, we'll be worshipping Jesus together again.

I hope Dorothy will be there too.

## *Connecting the Dots*

It not always about *what* you know, it's also *Who* you know.

- Who is Jesus? That's a good question. I'll let Him speak for Himself.

- The woman said, "I know that Messiah" (called Christ) "is coming. When he comes, he will explain everything to us." Then Jesus declared, "I, the one speaking to you—I am he." (John 4:25-26 NIV)

- Then Jesus declared, "I am the bread of life. Whoever comes to me will never go hungry, and whoever believes in me will never be thirsty." (John 6:35 NIV)

- But he continued, "You are from below; I am from above. You are of this world; I am not of this world." (John 8:23 NIV)

- Jesus said to her, "I am the resurrection and the life. The one who believes in me will live, even though they die; and whoever lives by believing in me will never die. Do you believe this?" (John 11:25-26 NIV)

- "You call me 'Teacher' and 'Lord,' and rightly so, for that is what I am." (John 13:13 NIV)

- Jesus answered, "I am the way and the truth and the life. No one comes to the Father except through me." (John 14:6 NIV)

Jesus doesn't leave any wiggle room when He speaks about who He is. As CS Lewis said, Jesus is either: a: the Lord; b: a lunatic; or c: a liar. I'll take A.

- A defining characteristic that sets the Kingdom of God apart from every other personal or worldly Kingdom is forgiveness. Dorothy had a real problem with forgiveness. Benny wanted the forgiveness that was part of the Kingdom. Dorothy seemed to stand on the outside, looking in.

- Then Peter came up and said to him, "Lord, how often will my brother sin against me, and I forgive him? As many as seven times?" Jesus said to him, "I do not say to you seven times, but seventy-seven times. Therefore the Kingdom of Heaven may be compared to a king who wished to settle accounts with his servants. When he began to settle, one was brought to him who owed him ten thousand talents. And since he could not pay, his master ordered him to be sold, with his wife and children and all that he had, and payment to be made. So the servant fell on his knees, imploring him, 'Have patience with me, and I will pay you everything.' And out of pity for him, the master of that servant released him and forgave him the debt. But when that same servant went out, he found one of his fellow servants who owed him a hundred denarii, and seizing him, he began to choke him, saying, 'Pay what you owe.' So his fellow servant fell down and pleaded with him, 'Have patience with me, and I will pay you.' He refused and went and put him in prison until he should pay the debt.
When his fellow servants saw what had taken place, they were greatly distressed, and they went and reported to their master all that had taken place. Then his master summoned him and said to him, 'You

wicked servant! I forgave you all that debt because you pleaded with me. And should not you have had mercy on your fellow servant, as I had mercy on you?'" (Matthew 18:21-33 ESV)

Dorothy resembled this old and memorable quote: "Unforgiveness is like taking poison and waiting for your enemy to die." In this case it was her husband.

- Benny was looking forward to Heaven. God has His Kingdom waiting for us in Heaven (this is the "not just yet" Kingdom). And then there is His Kingdom here on earth (the "now" Kingdom). You can't get into the one upstairs until you go through the one down here.

- Jesus replied, "Very truly I tell you, no one can see the Kingdom of God unless they are born again." (John 3:3 NIV)

- Benny worshipped because Jesus gave him hope of being resurrected and hope of Heaven. Not the kind of hope that says "I wish" something good will happen. But the sure and living hope of Heaven.

- Praise be to the God and Father of our Lord Jesus Christ! In his great mercy he has given us new birth into a living hope through the resurrection of Jesus Christ from the dead, and into an inheritance that can never perish, spoil or fade. This inheritance is kept in Heaven for you (1 Peter 1:3-4 NIV).

The blind shall see. The lame shall walk. The deaf shall hear. Blessed be the name of the Lord!

# Chapter 8
# Here is Grace

As I slid down the long stair rail of life, Hal was just a sliver in my butt. He ended up forcing me out of that little country church. Unfortunately, that's a common tale for pastors. At the time, it hurt. But I healed quickly and moved on. Jesus helped me put things in perspective.

Next stop? Carrie and I were house parents at a maternity home. For the next couple of years, Carrie and I cared for pregnant teenaged girls.

Can you say drama? Each one was a little drama queen in her own right. The girls' behind-the-scenes stories shocked me far more than many of the crimes told to me by inmates.

The big difference between the drama in the prison and the drama in the maternity home? In prison ministry, I got to go home at the end of the day.

There were perks, however. Midnight runs to KFC. Ben & Jerry's on demand. Waffles for breakfast.

The girls became like daughters to Carrie and me, and that was the best part of this job. One girl gave me the honorary title of "fake dad," which she still calls me today. She even named her little boy after me. She and Carrie are the best of friends to this day. Each girl we cared for was precious to us.

Penny was an inner-city eighth grader who came to us two months pregnant. How do you afford a rock-and-roll lifestyle at age thirteen? For starters, you run with a high-dollar drug dealer. This was Penny's routine: openly defying her parents so she could enjoy the bling and glamour of white lines and clubbing.

Take a walk on the wild side. When Penny was only twelve years old, her adult drug-dealing boyfriend flew them to New York City so they could go clubbing on New Year's Eve. She had many stories like that one.

Penny looked twenty-one. She was thirteen when she came to us. At only five foot two, Penny may have been slight, but she had the will of a mule and the spirit of a prized racehorse. These qualities made her hard to handle. They also made her truly exceptional.

Penny's dad dropped her off at the maternity home, a posh 4,000-square-foot home built for the purpose of ministering to young girls in crisis pregnancy. He left the moment he'd dropped her off. That was the second sign of trouble between them. The first sign was his pregnant thirteen-year-old daughter.

People are always putting it on for religious leaders. Church folk do it for their pastors. Inmates do it for their chaplains. Maternity home girls do it for their house parents.

Over the years, Penny learned to be real with people, which is remarkable, considering all the scheming she did at such a young age.

During the years Penny lived with us, a number of other girls came and went. Some lasted a whole day.

One girl asked to sleep in the same room as Penny because she was used to sleeping in her mom's bed. She was seventeen. I know, right? Then she cried herself to sleep when we said no. Sorry, sweetie, you have a room all to yourself now. Her tantrum lasted for two days until mommy and daddy drove twelve hours to take her home. In hindsight, we see God graced us all in the way it played out.

I love God's providence. Especially when He makes life simpler.

Being really nerdy comes in handy when you're a house parent. I don't know how else to say it—Carrie and I are just plain nerdy. Every nerd knows other nerds are fun. To non-nerds, though, not so much. For being a rowdy city girl beyond her years, Penny responded well to her new nerdy parents from the sticks.

We were not at all like her mom and dad at home. For starters, we were fun. We danced the oompa-loompa dance to Charlie and the Chocolate Factory. We carved out the snow in the front yard so the pregnant girls could lay on their bellies. We made sure that, in addition to eating healthy, they had plenty of processed sugar after nine p.m.

Unlike a lot of the families these girls came from, we had fun. And we treated them with respect. I learned from the prison cops that if you want respect, you give respect. This universal principle works for parents too. Penny immediately responded to Carrie and me. And a lifelong friendship started.

Our bonds with Penny tightened fast. That will happen with lots of doctor appointments together, midnight munchie runs, and processed sugar. But mostly those bonds grew because we listened during her emotion swings. Gentleness and calmness helped confused, vulnerable pregnant girls during the ups and downs. It made for ties that bind.

In case you are thinking Carrie and I are emotional giants, I need to let you know that, as soon as we were off duty, the first thing we did was go crazy. Snap. Bicker. Fuss. Blow the froth off a couple. It took two days just to regain our emotional sanity after every ten-day shift.

Bonding happened underneath all these emotions with the girls. Bonding and adoption. Penny was "adopted" into our family without even realizing it.

Ironically, she needed some serious love to help her decide to whether to keep her baby or place her for adoption.

More ironically, God sought to adopt Penny as His little girl too.

Imagine starting the eighth grade in September, knowing your baby was due in April. Add Penny's personality into the mix, and that's the recipe for some big-time drama.

I didn't know who God was ministering to more in this sea of emotion—Penny or me. She was one to rock the boat. Penny was like lots of teens. Power struggles. "No, I won't eat that!" "The rules don't apply to me!" "That's not fair!" Hormones on parade.

Crying was common. Most often, crying pointed to confusion. Inner conflict. Guilt. What do I do with my baby? How can I give up my baby? How can I take care of my baby? If I give her up for adoption, how do I deal with my guilt? How can I go into the ninth grade with a newborn? If my parents won't accept me now, how will they accept me when I come home with a baby they disapprove of? Couldn't my drug-dealer boyfriend help me?

Heavy, I know.

This kind of inner turmoil made Penny susceptible to being nurtured. She was desperate. Carrie became the mom Penny missed for a few rough years. If God had a dictionary and you looked up the word "Mom," you'd see Carrie's picture beside it. They spent many hours together with tears on each other's shoulders. Carrie loved all the girls through their struggles.

Penny was abandoned by her real mom on another continent and then abandoned by her father to the maternity home. Though we never spoke the word "adoption," that's what Penny experienced.

One night, after a really healthy, nerdy dinner that included asparagus and other ugly green foods, the other girls cleaned up. ("Aw, do we have to?" "You do if you want root beer floats." Actually, most of the time the girls enjoyed the love and structure. The green food—not so much.)

Since Penny had the evening off cleanup duty, the opportunity presented itself for her to hear the gospel. We had a comfy counseling area in the house. Penny and I sat down to talk. After months in the house, Penny trusted me. She knew I genuinely cared for her. This wild city girl even learned to like my nerdy jokes.

This evening, however, she wasn't in the mood for laughing. She was overwhelmed and the tears came quickly. This was the night her question of questions opened her heart and led her to her adoption by her Heavenly Father.

Penny was already sobbing when she sat in the chair next to mine. "How do I give up my baby?"

The answer rested in Jesus and His gospel. I answered Penny's question with a question. "What would you say is the essence of love?" That's a tough question. Especially for a thirteen-year-old.

"I don't know. What?" she said.

My answer was a simple example. "God gave His Son."

"But gave Him to do what?"

The answer? "To sacrifice Himself."

I explained to Penny that in God's sacrifice, we can see His love.

I explained that placing her baby for adoption would not be an unloving thing. Quite the opposite. If God sacrificed His Son to show His love for Penny, then her "sacrifice" to release her baby to adoptive parents would be an act of love too.

At that moment, God's love became clear to her. Penny saw God's love in the sacrifice of His Son. She could relate to what God gave up for her.

In that divine moment, Penny responded to the Holy Spirit. She accepted the love of God for herself. And in that same moment, she unselfishly decided to place her baby for adoption. God's love abounded.

It took a few hours for the mix of emotions to subside. Receiving Christ. Deciding to place your baby. This is really heavy stuff all at once. Tears of joy would give way to the reality of placing her child. This emotional back and forth finally led to fatigue.

Joy comes in the morning.

I'm sure Penny forgot about the root beer floats that night. But not about her salvation. Not about the freedom of love and sacrifice.

Talk about someone who understands love, sacrifice, and grace—that's Penny. She proved it when she presented her baby daughter to the family who adopted the infant. "Here is Grace," she said. She named her baby Grace!

First we adopt Penny. Then God adopts Penny. Then a family adopts Grace.

Pixie dust, magic pumpkins, and dopey dwarfs make for good stories, but nothing beats the grace of God in real life. Sometimes life resembles fairy tales.

Penny's father never came back to take her home after she delivered her baby.

She continued to live with Carrie and me after we left the maternity home ministry. That additional overdose of her father's rejection sent her reeling again. Penny would eventually move away from us and go to stay with her distant family. But she would come back to us, her adopted family.

Two years later she returned to us, expecting another baby.

While pregnant and living with us, she finished high school. Then she returned home to marry the daddy of her second child. A few years later, she finished beauty school. Then nursing school. She and her husband now have two more children. Talk about fairy tale endings ...

God's grace to Penny started a chain reaction of love.

Today Penny is a beautiful and poised young woman, married for years to her second child's father. Penny even took the initiative to reconcile with her own father. He is enjoying his grandkids. And Penny's mom who left her? They were also reunited. God's love turned life around for so many families. God's grace looks good on all who receive it.

Over the years, Penny has reunited with her daughter, Grace. Grace's adoptive parents have been lovingly supportive of Penny, adding to a wonderful "happily ever after." Praise God for His adopting grace!

## *Connecting the Dots*

- Every Christian has been adopted by God.

- Yet to all who did receive him, to those who believed in his name, he gave the right to become children of God— children born not of natural descent, nor of human decision or a husband's will, but born of God. (John 1:12-13 NIV)

- For those who are led by the Spirit of God are the children of God. The Spirit you received does not make you slaves, so that you live in fear again; rather, the Spirit you received brought about your adoption to sonship. And by him we cry, "Abba, Father." (Romans 8:14-15 NIV)

- See what great love the Father has lavished on us, that we should be called children of God! And that is what we are! (1 John 3:1 NIV)

- How does a teenaged girl who ran with drug dealers and got pregnant twice before graduating high school make it to adulthood and live a clean, healthy life? Love and perseverance are a powerful combination.

- Above all, love each other deeply, because love covers over a multitude of sins. (1 Peter 4:8 NIV)

- Let perseverance finish its work so that you may be mature and complete, not lacking anything. (James 1:4 NIV)

- As you know, we count as blessed those who have persevered. You have heard of Job's perseverance and have seen what the Lord finally brought about. The Lord is full of compassion and mercy. (James 5:11 NIV)

- This next verse not only sums up Penny's conversion, but it also connects the dots to her family.
- Therefore, if anyone is in Christ, the new creation has come: The old has gone, the new is here! All this is from God, who reconciled us to himself through Christ and gave us the ministry of reconciliation. (2 Corinthians 5:17-18 NIV)

For the Kingdom of God does not consist in talk but in power. (1 Corinthians 4:20 ESV)

# Chapter 9
# The Blessing of Fear

Being scared is not always a bad thing. Being scared can help you know when to run away from danger. Not knowing when to be afraid can have painful consequences.

A young girl I once met landed herself in prison because she didn't know when to be afraid. But when God gave her a second chance to be scared, she found Christ.

As a maternity home house dad, I had the privilege of preaching at various churches in my area. One Sunday, I was a guest preacher at a new church near the home. We took the girls in our care to worship.

This place didn't feel at all churchy. The parking lot was dirt and gravel, with lots of puddles and mud. The inside of the building was stark.

When we went through the door, the first thing we noticed was the silence. Very awkward. The people at this church didn't seem to mind the silence, though.

Many different types of folks sat there. Nerds, rednecks, and knuckleheads. Homeless folks. Students. Moms and dads. Old folks. A few professional types. Mostly blue-collar trailer-park folk. Salt-of-the-earth types.

Not many folks there had especially good greeting skills, which explains the silence at first. But if you started a conversation, the hard part was getting them to stop. There was no shortage of smiles. I immediately liked these people. As more folks trickled in, laughter and noisy conversations replaced the silence.

I like a good mix. And these broken people seemed receptive to people unlike themselves. These are ingredients for a move of God.

The church filled up fast. But I noticed about four rows were roped off with no signs indicating who should sit there. As a guest, I refrained from asking. Then, about five minutes before we were to begin, about thirty teenaged girls came in through the side door and filled the empty chairs. They were all from a local detention center. The center bused them to this church every Sunday.

The girls were nervous. But the congregation was used to the weekly busload. There wasn't the typical "look the other way" from the congregation when the girls walked in. Just the opposite. I saw lots of smiles and eye contact but zero judgmental stares as the girls came in

and sat down. Even though those people weren't all that skilled at starting conversations, they were quite good at making the girls feel welcome. Good job, nerds!

I was excited to see the girls from the detention center. My prison chaplain experience helped me know how to connect with them.

Worship was longer than I was used to. I enjoyed that. So did everyone else. It wasn't polished but it was sincere. And the longer we sang, the more the girls enjoyed it. You could see it. If you are a young teen in a detention facility, being made to feel self-conscious was part of the routine. When something like unpolished, authentic worship happens, it helps you let your guard down a little. You have an opportunity with God.

When your guard is down, you can deal with fear.

After the singing, it was time for me to preach. I spoke about the time Jesus sat in the boat with His disciples and how He calmed the wind and the waves. I talked about the disciples' fear and Jesus's power. I told the folks that Jesus could overcome any fear through any storm.

But I also said that if you did not trust Jesus with your soul for your eternity, then there was an eternal storm on the horizon on the other side of this life. A storm that was impossible to weather without Him. That eternal storm would be Hell. Literally.

You don't hear much about Hell these days.

Once a chaplain friend of mine said you could say anything to someone as long as they knew you loved them. I made sure to speak to that congregation about my days in prison ministry. When folks heard how I ministered to drunks, murderers, and sex offenders, I think they understood I accepted folks. That helped break the ice on the subject of Hell.

If my seminary professor had been there to evaluate my sermon, I would have been embarrassed. My talk missed the main point of the text I was teaching. I tried to connect some spiritual dots, but they were too spread out. Good thing God makes up for all that I lack. And He did it in a big way.

After I spoke, I invited anyone who had a question to talk to me privately. Two of the detention girls came to speak with Carrie and me. One of the girls was a

Christian. Jill, her friend was not. Jill needed her friend beside her. She was scared. And not just to talk to me.

She was scared of many things as she entered that church building. She was self-conscious. Shy and ashamed. She was scared of being rejected.

But one thing she wasn't scared about that day was asking a spiritual question about something she was unfamiliar with.

Jill had never considered Hell before. Didn't know a thing about it. She was scared of going to Hell.

It's a good thing Carrie was there. She was able to hold the young girl's hand and comfort her as she told us her life story.

The tears really started to flow when she asked more about Hell. This was her first time learning about this place. Jill wasn't just scared. She was terrified. Trembling. She had to stop numerous times to wipe her eyes and blow her nose.

I talked to her about faith in Christ and reassured her about His promises to deliver her from this awful place.

When I asked her if she wanted to believe, she didn't hesitate. She confessed her faith in Christ right then and there. No prompting. Jill's prayer was awkward and authentic. Just like this church. God is okay with awkward and authentic. After a few more minutes, the tears went away and she started laughing. She was so relieved to escape Hell.

After the joy and the hugs, I told her about counting the cost to follow Jesus. She was all for it. "How could I not?" she exclaimed in her squirrely teenaged voice.

We had plenty of time to talk. No one was in a hurry.

Instead of joining everyone else for lunch at the church, Carrie and I continued to listen to Jill. She talked about her family. It wasn't pretty. She told us about the abuse and the guilt she had a hard time getting rid of. Hearing that, I explained some things about Jesus and his gospel that I had not said during my sermon.

Every sermon should point to Jesus and His cross in some way. Even though I felt as if I had blown it, God gave me a second chance to tell Jill more personally about the cross.

Jill was having a very difficult time with guilt. I explained that her faith would not only save her from Hell but that Jesus would forgive her sins too. That His blood and forgiveness would not only keep her from Hell, but they would also give her freedom from guilt.

The three of us huddled together at the front of the church. Crying. Laughing. Praying.

After hearing about His cross and blood, Jill looked up at all of us gathered around, her eyes wide with a look of amazement. "What? You mean my sins are forgiven too?"

The faucets turned on again. More tears of joy. Then more hugs.

When we started to tell her about the Holy Spirit, she got all excited again and said, "You mean there's more?"

While the other girls were loading up into the bus, Jill kept asking, "Who is this Spirit? What's He all about?" I asked her friend to tell her more about the Holy Spirit. Her friend smiled at Carrie and me and said she would try to explain more of God's grace.

When the freedom of God's forgiveness was spoken,

Jill grabbed hold of Jesus as if He was saving her from a terrible storm. She said she could relate to those men in the boat with Jesus. If we'd had all afternoon, she would have soaked it all in nonstop. I have no doubt.

I'll never forget Jill's tears of faith when she told me good-bye at the side door.

I went back to the church after that Sunday and saw more scared little girls. But I never saw Jill again.

That scared kid was willing to follow Jesus solely on the promise that He would save her from Hell. If only that kind of devotion were more common.

Fear can be a good thing. It can compel us to look up. To cry out. To see God.

I have heard it said that "Do not be afraid" is one of the most frequent assurances in the Bible. On the flip side, Jesus said, "Be afraid of the one who can destroy both soul and body in Hell."

Maybe this is a warning that more folks need to hear. It's good to be afraid. It can keep you out of trouble. And not just on this side of eternity.

Thank God for the many ways He makes good on His grace and mercy. Like no Hell. Like forgiveness. Like His Holy Spirit.

God reached down and scared the Hell out of that little girl.

## *Connecting the Dots*

- Fear can be a good thing. Too many people are in prison because they were not afraid. Not fearful enough to walk away. We should be afraid of some physical things. We should be afraid of some spiritual things.

- Be afraid of the One who can destroy both soul and body in Hell. Are not two sparrows sold for a penny? Yet not one of them will fall to the ground outside your Father's care. And even the very hairs of your head are all numbered. So don't be afraid; you are worth more than many sparrows. (Matthew 10:28-31 NIV)

- There is no fear in love. But perfect love drives out fear, because fear has to do with punishment. (1 John 4:18 NIV)

God's grace has many facets. My time was limited with that young girl who saw just a couple of facets and believed. Unlike church that day, here in this chapter I have the luxury to slow down and show how the Bible reveals more of the facets of God's grace.

### Grace Before the Cross

- God's election is an expression of His grace.

- He has saved us and called us to a holy life—not because of anything we have done but because of his own purpose and grace. *This grace was given us in Christ Jesus before the beginning of time.* (2 Timothy 1:9 NIV)

- For he chose us in him *before the creation of the world* to be holy and blameless in his sight. In love he predestined us for adoption to sonship through Jesus Christ, in accordance with his pleasure and will— to the praise of his glorious grace, which he has freely given us in the One he loves. (Ephesians 1:4-6 NIV)

- In him we were also chosen, *having been predestined* according to the plan of him who works out everything in conformity with the purpose of his will. (Ephesians 1:11)

## Grace Given On the Cross

- Jesus forgives our sins.
- In him we have redemption through his blood, the forgiveness of sins, in accordance with the riches of God's grace. (Ephesians 1:7 NIV)

- Jesus's sacrifice was an offering to God to pay for the indebtedness our sin caused.
- And though the Lord makes his life an offering for sin, he will see his offspring and prolong his days, and the will of the Lord will prosper in his hand. (Isaiah 53:10 NIV)

- Jesus was a ransom to reconcile sinners to God.
- For even the Son of Man did not come to be served, but to serve, and to give his life as a ransom for many. (Mark 10:45 NIV)

- Jesus' perfect obedience in going to the cross is now the Christian's standing before God.

- Consequently, just as one trespass resulted in condemnation for all people, so also one righteous act resulted in justification and life for all people. For just as through the disobedience of the one man the many were made sinners, so also through the obedience of the one man the many will be made righteous. (Romans 5:18-19 NIV)

- On the cross, Jesus substituted Himself for the sinner, not wanting him to go through suffering.

- For Christ also suffered once for sins, the righteous for the unrighteous, to bring you to God. He was put to death in the body but made alive in the Spirit. (1 Peter 3:18 NIV)

- Jesus is the sinner's redemption (He pays for the sinners' salvation with His blood).

- For he has rescued us from the dominion of darkness and brought us into the Kingdom of the Son he loves, in whom we have redemption, the forgiveness of sins. (Colossians 1:13-14 NIV)

- He [Jesus] did not enter by means of the blood of goats and calves; but he entered the Most Holy Place once for all by his own blood, thus obtaining eternal redemption. (Hebrews 9:12 NIV)

- Christ redeemed us from the curse of the law by becoming a curse for us, for it is written: "Cursed is

- everyone who is hung on a pole." (Galatians 3:13 NIV)
- Israel, put your hope in the Lord, for with the Lord is unfailing love and with him is full redemption. (Psalm 130:7 NIV)

- On the cross, Jesus took upon Himself God's hatred of our sins.
- Since we have now been justified by his blood, how much more shall we be saved from God's wrath through him! (Romans 5:9 NIV)
- For God did not appoint us to suffer wrath but to receive salvation through our Lord Jesus Christ. (1 Thessalonians 5:9 NIV)
- [He became] a merciful and faithful high priest in the service of God, to make propitiation for the sins of the people [propitiation means to appease anger or wrath]. (Hebrews 2:17 ESV)
- There is therefore now no condemnation for those who are in Christ Jesus. (Romans 8:1 ESV)

- Because of Jesus and the cross, there was a "great exchange." He took men's sin and, in exchange, gave us God's righteousness.
- For Christ is the end of the law for righteousness to everyone who believes. (Romans 10:4 ESV)
- For our sake he made him to be sin who knew no sin, so that in him we might become the righteousness of God. (2 Corinthians 5:21 ESV)

- The next day he saw Jesus coming toward him, and said, "Behold, the Lamb of God, who takes away the sin of the world!" (John 1:29 ESV)

- Because Jesus went to the cross, a sinner can be spared from Hell by receiving Jesus by faith.

- For God so loved the world that he gave his one and only Son, that whoever believes in him shall not perish but have eternal life. (John 3:16 NIV)

- "There was a rich man who was clothed in purple and fine linen and who feasted sumptuously every day. And at his gate was laid a poor man named Lazarus, covered with sores, who desired to be fed with what fell from the rich man's table. Moreover, even the dogs came and licked his sores. The poor man died and was carried by the angels to Abraham's side. The rich man also died and was buried, and in Hades, being in torment, he lifted up his eyes and saw Abraham far off and Lazarus at his side. And he called out, 'Father Abraham, have mercy on me, and send Lazarus to dip the end of his finger in water and cool my tongue, for I am in anguish in this flame.' But Abraham said, 'Child, remember that you in your lifetime received your good things, and Lazarus in like manner bad things; but now he is comforted here, and you are in anguish. And besides all this, between us and you a great chasm has been fixed, in order that those who would pass from here to you may not be able, and none may cross from there to us.' And he said, 'Then I beg you, father, to send him to my father's house—for I have five brothers—so that he may warn them, lest they also come into this place of torment.' But Abraham said, 'They have Moses and the Prophets; let them hear them.' And he said, 'No, father Abraham, but if someone goes to them from the dead, they will repent.' He said to him, 'If they do not hear Moses and the Prophets, neither will they be convinced if someone should rise from the dead.'" (Luke 16:19-31 ESV)

- God gives a sinner faith to believe in Him and His sovereign gift of grace.

- For it is by grace you have been saved, through faith— and this is not from yourselves, it is the gift of God. (Ephesians 2:8 NIV)

- One of those listening was a woman from the city of Thyatira named Lydia, a dealer in purple cloth. She was a worshiper of God. The Lord opened her heart to respond to Paul's message. (Acts 16:14 NIV)

- Through Jesus and His cross alone, the sinner can be justified before God.

- Therefore, since we have been justified through faith, we have peace with God through our Lord Jesus Christ. (Romans 5:1 NIV)

- Know that a person is not justified by the works of the law, but by faith in Jesus Christ. So we, too, have put our faith in Christ Jesus that we may be justified by faith in Christ and not by the works of the law, because by the works of the law no one will be justified. (Galatians 2:16 NIV)

**God not only supplies grace to sinners; He applies grace to sinners as well.**

- He makes spiritually dead sinners spiritually alive.

- I will give you a new heart and put a new spirit in you; I will remove from you your heart of stone and give you a heart of flesh. And I will put my Spirit in you and move you to follow my decrees and be careful to keep my laws. (Ezekiel 36:26-27 NIV)

- Flesh gives birth to flesh, but the Spirit gives birth to spirit. (John 3:6 NIV)

- He saved us, not because of righteous things we had done, but because of his mercy. He saved us through the washing of rebirth and renewal by the Holy Spirit, whom he poured out on us generously through Jesus Christ our Savior. (Titus 3:5-6 NIV)


- God gives the sinner the gift of His Holy Spirit when he receives Christ by faith.

- Peter replied, "Repent and be baptized, every one of you, in the name of Jesus Christ for the forgiveness of your sins. And you will receive the gift of the Holy Spirit." (Acts 2:38 NIV)

- And you also were included in Christ, when you heard the message of truth, the gospel of your salvation. When you believed, you were marked in him with a seal, the promised Holy Spirit. (Ephesians 1:13 NIV)

- We know that we live in him and he lives in us because

he has given us his Spirit. (1 John 4:13 GW)

- God has adopted sinners and takes them as His children.
- "I will be a Father to you, and you will be my sons and daughters, says the Lord Almighty." (2 Corinthians 6:18 NIV)
- But when the fullness of time had come, God sent forth his Son, born of a woman, born under the law, to redeem those who were under the law, so that we might receive adoption as sons. And because you are sons, God has sent the Spirit of his Son into our hearts. (Galatians 4:4-6 NIV)

## Future Grace Awaits Too

- For we know that if the earthly tent we live in is destroyed, we have a building from God, an eternal house in Heaven, not built by human hands. (2 Corinthians 5:1 NIV)
- Do not let your hearts be troubled. Trust in God. Trust also in me. In my Father's house are many rooms. If it were not so I would have told you. I am going there to prepare a place for you. And if I go there to prepare a place for you, I will come back and take you to be with me, that you may be where I am also. (John 14:1-3)
- Where, O death is your victory? Where, O death is your sting? But thanks be to God! He gives us the victory through our Lord Jesus Christ. (1 Corinthians 15:55, 57 NIV)

- Add up all these facets of God's grace, and what do you have? Reconciliation with God.

- We also rejoice in God through our Lord Jesus Christ, through whom we have now received reconciliation. (Romans 5:11 ESV)

- For God was pleased to have all his fullness dwell in him [Jesus], and through him to reconcile himself to all things, whether things on earth or things in Heaven, by making peace through his blood, shed on the cross. (Colossians 1:19-20 NIV)

After looking at all this grace, I can understand why Jesus says, "Do not be afraid."

## Chapter 10
## Bad Credit? No Credit? No Problem!

I'm a spiritual junkie. I can't help but tell people about Jesus.

After the maternity home ministry, I took a gig as a hospice chaplain. Most people expect a chaplain to be spiritually neutral. But how does a person with deep convictions remain impartial? If a good chaplain is a spiritually neutral guy, then I stunk at it.

It was a privilege to comfort the dying and to minister to the ones they would leave behind.

It was an opportunity to win souls for Christ. To give hope. To be a hospice chaplain is to walk in a very fertile field.

As far as professional hospice chaplains go, one of my major shortcomings was my inability to grasp the computerized medical charting. I was one notch below a trained monkey.

My lousy computer skills notwithstanding, this was one of the most exciting spiritual arenas I've ever been in. There is so much spiritual activity going on in souls who are about to come to the last fork in their road. Helping a desperate person is something I've always been passionate about.

During his last days, Bob was a hospice patient in a very upscale assisted-living facility. He was quite likable. Because of his medical condition, he spoke very slowly and softly. Asking a question could easily take a full minute.

Before he spoke, a wry smile always formed on his face, which made him easy to listen to. Bob was engaging. It was clear that during his earlier years he'd been high energy, a Type A personality. He still showed signs of this in his final season.

Everyone has their own unique way they want to be listened to. Bob was no exception. Nurses and social workers often came to visit and ask questions while I was with him. But because Bob was so slow to answer, they often interrupted him or assumed an answer and moved on to the next question. Then they repeated the process.

This frustrated Bob because he knew how to communicate and still could. He simply required more time and patience from his listeners. As I watched these interactions, it helped me know how to communicate with Bob.

When people are in hospice care, time changes. Before a terminal diagnosis, folks seem to think they have plenty of time. But after the diagnosis, the future can seem like trying to catch a waterfall in a bucket. End-of-life urgency and a sense of being overwhelmed can set in. This is what happened to Bob.

I began by asking him about his immediate comfort. I then moved on to ask about his life. Bob welcomed our conversations about his past.

Bob and I got on the subject of pain. We talked about the pain in the soul and in the body. There was definite pain in Bob's soul. It dogged him every bit as much as the pain in his body. He said he felt the two were connected.

We processed through the idea that his soul could be free of pain apart from the pain in his body. At first he didn't believe this was possible.

So I told him a few stories about Christian martyrs who were burned at the stake while rejoicing at the prospect of meeting God. They rejoiced because their souls were free. This increased Bob's spiritual curiosity. He'd never heard such stories before.

I got to know Bob. I listened. He let me in. When it was my turn to talk, I told him Jesus's parable of the unforgiving servant. I told the story in simple, everyday terms. A man who owes a bundle to the company he works for goes to the owner, pleading he will forgive his debt. Makes all kinds of promises. The boss forgives the debt entirely. Off the books. Then the forgiven man turns right around and chokes a fellow worker, demanding the ten bucks the other guy owes him. As a result, the man who was forgiven the huge debt was now thrown into prison for his hypocrisy. A prison where he is bound by his own unwillingness to forgive.

I would like to take credit for the effect this parable had on Bob. But I can't. It was all God.

Bob immediately related to this parable because he also was in a prison, bound by unforgiveness.

By his own confession, Bob told me that early in his life he loaned money to his brother, James, to help him secure a real estate contract. After the land deal closed, they both would gain a profit of $300,000. Through no fault of James's, a third party threw a wrench in the flywheel, and the deal fell through. Bob thought James had betrayed him. But before there was any chance for the brothers to work things out financially, James died suddenly. Bob was left with both the debt and the bitterness of not being able to reconcile over all that happened. And for decades Bob felt cheated by his brother and lived in the prison of unforgiveness.

Bob agreed to let me pray over him. That was where I left things that day—with Bob feeling restless about his spiritual condition. Unforgiveness over his brother. Still hanging on to decades of bitterness with no prospect for reconciliation.

It was as if the Holy Spirit knew just what Bob needed to hear.

The next day, I didn't feel like going to see Bob again. I was tired and emotionally spent. I was in no mood to be an evangelist. Was it out of obedience that I turned the car around and headed toward the assisted-living facility? I don't think so. Again, I'll give credit to the Holy Spirit.

After I changed directions and headed over to see Bob, I thought about the movie *Amadeus*. It's a movie about Mozart and a rival composer named Salieri. Salieri was riddled with guilt for thinking he'd had a hand in Mozart's death. When the priest came to ease Salieri's guilt, he told Salieri to offer him his confession.

I was driving over to ask Bob for his confession. A good thing for a man on his deathbed.

Like Salieri, Bob was eager to confess. He described a selfish life void of God. He confessed that he did not believe in God. I knew from experience that I needed to fight the urge to debate this subject. Not only that, the guy was dying. I didn't have the heart to argue with him. The Bible reminded me that men do indeed know God is real.

I did speak to Bob about his conscience. I got a clear

sense that God was convicting him. Then I added fuel to his convicted soul. I asked him why he would let me pray the day before, but then tell me there was no God? I meant it as a serious question. This got to him. I let it get to him.

Because Bob had trouble speaking and our conversations were painfully slow, I had time to think through my every word and thought before speaking. I made them count.

Throughout his life, Bob was a high-powered entrepreneur. Knowing this, I explained the differences between the economies of God and the economy of men (spiritually speaking).

Men come to God offering "this for that." God's economy, I told him, was upside down and inside out from what we expect. God comes to us offering free grace, with Christ paying our debts. I told him Jesus is the "gold standard" of God's economy.

Bob connected with this business terminology. No Christianese. Just simple stuff. Then I told him God's economy of grace is freely given through Christ on the cross.

I thought I was observing Bob correctly, and later my assessment proved true. He was getting it. Believing it. Receiving it. It was amazing to watch. God was melting and changing Bob's heart of stone into a receiving, believing heart right before my eyes.

So I told him the gospel again, this time with something he could relate to: the parable of the workers in the field. The ones hired last got paid the same as those hired first. As a business owner, he would understand. Spiritually, God's grace was becoming understandable as well. I could see the lights turning on.

"Christ paid your debt with His own blood," I said.

Bob saw himself as the last worker in line. Days away from death, he knew exactly what Jesus meant. I didn't have to connect the dots for him.

"What do I do with all this?" he asked.

"The response is simple. Fall on Christ. Fall on His mercy. Receive Christ by faith."

"Faith, huh?" he said in a low, reflective, almost inaudible tone. His response slowly grew into delight, then pleasant surprise. Then he seemed almost amused.

Bob had admitted earlier that he had never prayed in his life. Now I asked him to pray. For about thirty seconds, he bowed his head in complete silence. Bob was praying for the first time in his life.

He received Christ. I could hardly believe it. It was glorious! Supernatural.

That half of a minute seemed like five minutes to me. All I could think about was Jack, the inmate who'd repeated my salvation prayer and used my own words to con me. I didn't want this to happen with Bob. That's why I asked him to pray by himself.

After those precious seconds, Bob lifted his head and said to me, "You got yourself a convert."

I asked him straight up, "Are you BS-ing me, Bob?"

And in a slow, matter-of-fact tone and without any change of expression, he simply said, "No."

I stayed with Bob and we talked about life and death. About a half hour later, he said to me, "Give this Christian a drink of water."

I was shocked. Knowing his past contempt for Christians and Christianity, his words were nothing short of astonishing. He'd confessed to being a Christian!

And I had seen the work of the Holy Spirit. A lifetime of selfishly rejecting God had changed in a twinkling of an eye. God is simply amazing.

Regeneration is like the story of Frankenstein, bringing forth life from death.

After this visit, I immediately went home and began reading about conversions. Regeneration has long been one of my favorite topics to study and teach. I came across an old book entitled *M'Cheyne Memoirs* that contained sermons from a nineteenth-century preacher, Robert Murray M'Cheyne. (Note: All dead Presbyterian Scots are worth reading over and over.) Here is what M'Cheyne said about conversion.

*The conversion of a soul is by far the most remarkable event in the history of the world, although many of you do not care about it. It is the object that attracts the eyes of holy angels to the spot where it takes place. It is the object which the Father's eyes rest upon with tenderness and delight. This work in the soul is what brings greater glory to the Father, Son, and Spirit, more than all the other works of God. It is far more wonderful than all the works of art. There is nothing that can equal it.*

The next day was only slightly less amazing. As Bob and I spoke, he continued to confess his sins. He was quite specific. He commented to me about himself in third person. "You know, Bob never thought about anything except Bob his entire life."

He came to grips with himself. I'll be honest; after all

Bob told me about his selfish life, what I was now hearing was simply jaw-dropping.

After more talk about his physical condition, I asked Bob what else he would like to talk about. Again his answer was priceless. "You mean regarding Christ?"

I laughed. He was thinking about Jesus.

Bob had been in hospice less than a week, and not only had the pain in his body left, but his soul had also found healing and peace in Christ.

The following days held some memorable events. Bob asked me, "Now that I'm a Christian, now what?" What a great question! A dying man asks what to do with his newfound Christianity. I asked if he had ever worshipped God. He had not.

I located a hymnal and sang for him. He thoroughly enjoyed it. After that I put on some mellow Christian worship music. Seeing him worshipping along with the music felt like watching a friend see the mountains for the first time.

A man who had rejected God now worshipped Him. That's transformation.

On my next visit, Bob surprised me again. Out of the blue, and after a long silence, he prayed this prayer out loud, "I'm not very smart. This situation is out of my hands and into Yours, Lord. If You would help me, I would appreciate it."

I reached for my pen to write down his words. Then I started to cry.

Speaking only thirty to forty-five words per minute made this speech all the more powerful.

I told him that when we boast, we boast in the Lord.

He looked at me with confusion. Rightly so for a new Christian. I briefly explained that we are to give God His due for our salvation.

Bob was tracking with me. "You and I both swing in the lower half and we give Him the credit." By lower half I believe Bob meant down here on earth. He understood my words about giving credit to God and about His power to save.

"We give Him the credit." Those were Bob's last words.

I went to see him the next day. I was shocked to see his condition had deteriorated so quickly. He drifted in and out of consciousness.

Bob passed less than a week later. All in all, my conversations with Bob spanned only a week.

For the Type A personality man, it was the most productive week of his life.

After one of my last visits with Bob, I called and left a phone message with his daughter, who lived out of state. Again, sovereignty ran rampant that day. As I left the upscale facility where Bob was getting his care, I ran into his daughter in the lobby.

I told her of her father's conversion. She is a Christian and told me of her and her church's many prayers for her dad. She was overjoyed.

After Bob's passing, I was pleased to conduct his memorial service. I told his friends and family that Bob was one of the last to get paid. Naturally, they were shocked. They never thought they'd see him cashing a check from Jesus. Until the last couple weeks of his life, Bob never thought of it either.

## *Connecting the Dots*

- Bob's conversion aligns with the following parable of the workers in the field.

- '"For the Kingdom of Heaven is like a landowner who went out early in the morning to hire workers for his vineyard. He agreed to pay them a denarius for the day and sent them into his vineyard.

  About nine in the morning he went out and saw others standing in the marketplace doing nothing. He told them, 'You also go and work in my vineyard, and I will pay you whatever is right.' So they went.

  He went out again about noon and about three in the afternoon and did the same thing. About five in the afternoon he went out and found still others standing around. He asked them, 'Why have you been standing here all day long doing nothing?'

  'Because no one has hired us,' they answered.

  He said to them, 'You also go and work in my vineyard.'

  When evening came, the owner of the vineyard said to his foreman, 'Call the workers and pay them their wages, beginning with the last ones hired and going on to the first.'

  The workers who were hired about five in the afternoon came and each received a denarius. So when those came who were hired first, they expected to receive more. But each one of them also received a denarius. When they received it, they began to grumble against the landowner. 'These who were hired last worked only one hour,' they said, 'and you have made them equal to us who have borne the burden of the work and the heat of the day.'

But he answered one of them, 'I am not being unfair to you, friend. Didn't you agree to work for a denarius? Take your pay and go. I want to give the one who was hired last the same as I gave you. Don't I have the right to do what I want with my own money? Or are you envious because I am generous?'

So the last will be first, and the first will be last.'" (*Matthew 20:1-16 NIV*)

- Jesus is the gold standard of God's spiritual economy. Jesus paid it all.

- Knowing that you were ransomed from the futile ways inherited from your forefathers, not with perishable things such as silver or gold, but with the precious blood of Christ, like that of a lamb without blemish or spot. (1 Peter 1:18-19 ESV)

What do you do when you are on your deathbed and you don't have enough to pay your way into Heaven? You can't work. You can't borrow. You must receive or die.

# Chapter 11
# Discipleship Happens

We spend half our lives in transit, but that's just the way God plans it. I never planned on ending up back in Iowa, pastoring another church.

Sometimes I feel like a traveler God sends out to meet folks. Sort of a spiritual Doctor Who, only I'm limited to the time and space He allots me. But I still get to meet some amazing people. And I haven't run into any Daleks yet.

It seemed as if God was using my new church just to get me to Haiti. Actually, God assigned a young lady in that church to get me to Haiti. (Maybe she is Doctor Who.) Anyway, she sent a mere sixty dollars, in the name of the church I was pastoring, to a Haiti mission organization.

That mission organization called all the donating churches and asked the pastor if he would like a three-day tour of Haiti. This is how they networked. When they called me, I needed only a New York minute to say, "Yes!"

It was my first trip to Haiti. My first Third World experience. I wasn't sure what I would find. I had no idea how needy the people were there. I figured I'd just sniff around, spiritually speaking. You know … just lookin'. I've always liked spiritual adventures. Especially the kind with mystery.

The way things had fallen into place, I suspected God had something in store for me. I went with an open heart and an open mind.

But when I got there and smelled the garbage burning, saw the filth in the streets, drove for three hours in a riverbed they called a road, saw starving people, and experienced their desperation, I knew this was the place for me.

I didn't know it until much later, but I was on an assignment. A mission from God.

In hindsight, I can see God was setting me on a path to intercept a specific man with the gospel. A man I had never seen or heard of.

On this mysterious journey to meet this man I did not know, I visited a Haitian orphanage. I had about an hour to kill while waiting for my guides to do some business with the orphanage director.

You can sit around only so long, exchanging toothy grins and dumb stares with adorable kids who don't speak your language.

So I started to sing. The children within hearing distance stopped their activities and acted as if I was an alien who came to earth and spoke their language.

I decided to sing the hymn I heard every Sunday in the Lithuanian Catholic church I grew up in. Remember? This was the church with the wine-stained carpet and the perverted janitor. Every Sunday, we closed Mass with "Holy God, We Praise Thy Name."

That's what I sang to the kids. Jaws dropped. Smiles widened. Joy happened. The kids were shocked. I knew one of their songs! I was shocked to hear that they knew all the verses. We connected. It was a blast. I was on the right path.

This being my first trip to Haiti, I wondered if I was

in the hands of God. I was.

Sometimes you can walk around being all spiritual and not even know it.

I was thrown together with three pastors on this trip. One was a frail old woman. One was a young buck new to ministry. The other was a cranky, fatigued, almost-retired pastor who was just looking for a change of scenery for a few days. I knew pretty quickly this ol' boy would be trouble. He didn't seem to appreciate rednecks or sound doctrine.

At the end of the day, we four pastors sat around the table at the guest house. Me and Young Buck saw eye to eye on the Bible. Our other two friends ... not so much.

The next day, we happy pastors toured a neighborhood with thousands of homes made of tarps, scraps, and garbage. Homes built just inches from one another. And no sanitation.

This neighborhood sat on top of a riverbank. From our location down to the river was about two hundred feet of garbage as far as the eye could see. And the stink? Holy cow! Huge hogs rooted through the garbage. The people lived there because they were close to a water supply.

The river, when it flowed, was a thick, muddy-brown color. It stunk too. It was so awful, I couldn't think of using this water for anything. But these were desperate people.

It was all surreal. Poverty like I've never seen. All these sights. The sounds. The stench. Later, when we found some breathable air, God gave me a most shocking revelation. My spiritual "sniffing around" in Haiti would lead me to an answer I had been seeking since I was a prison chaplain. Without this stinky location and the equally stinky attitude of my colleague, I may have missed it.

And that's when it happened. I saw the answer written in black vinyl letters in the back window of a Toyota pickup. "Seek first the Kingdom of God."

That's it! That's what I was seeing and smelling in Haiti—the Kingdom of God. Mercy to the poor. Joy in suffering. Food for the hungry. Faith of the oppressed. Forgiveness to a knucklehead. The gospel to the desperate.

The visible Kingdom of God right before my eyes.

Those theological concepts I had read about were suddenly realized in a neighborhood that looked and smelled like a garbage dump.

Some lessons are better caught than taught. This one certainly was.

Haiti is one of the most spiritual places on the planet. Christianity explodes there—I know because I saw it. On any given Sunday, you can drive down the streets of Port au Prince, a city of millions, and see people standing outside church buildings because there are not enough seats inside. Standing room only for church? In Haiti, that's common. In the Haitian countryside, you can find the next church down the road just by hearing the worshippers rejoice.

Here is a culture that is being spiritually transformed. So much so, I could see the Kingdom of God.

My first two days in Haiti were like spiritual nirvana. On the third day (that always sounds so spiritual, doesn't it?), I met Guinel.

Guinel was my intended mission.

Guinel is a simple man. A man with great compassion. Not highly educated at all. A family man. A resourceful man. A very honest man. A man with courage and vision. A stubborn man. A man who would become aware of his weaknesses. A people pleaser. A teachable man. A patient man.

He is a good husband and father. He's popular in his village. He's overly sensitive. He is the official-unofficial head of his village. He is one of thirteen children. The youngest boy. His family has lived in this primitive Haitian village called Kilbitè for three hundred years.

Kilbitè means stumble in Kreyol. No one knows the story behind the name. The village has no running water. No electricity. Tarp huts. A dirty stream runs through it.

I guess I'm a spiritual romantic, because when I saw this jungle village, I fell in love with it. And with the people. It was so picturesque. People lived in tarp huts on dirt floors. They bathed in the stream. They cooked over primitive charcoal. Voodoo crosses hung everywhere.

Before I connect a few more dots and tell you more about God, Guinel, and discipleship, I must tell you how God set this scene for this divine meet.

Patrick and Eric are Haitians who were traveling on the Haiti Highway, Route National 1, heading north out of Port au Prince to Cabaret, Haiti. There was a riot in the middle of the road. They could drive no further. Burning tires made the road impassable. Gunshots kept everyone away in fear.

That's when Guinel showed up to rescue them.

Guinel introduced himself to Patrick and Eric and offered them a safe place and a meal. His village is a quarter mile back, in the jungle off the highway. They stayed with Guinel until things cooled off. A friendship started.

God used a riot as a detour to arrange a divine appointment.

Patrick and Eric were my tour guides when Pastor Cranky and I first toured Haiti. They introduced me to Guinel on this trip.

Fast forward six months. I'm with Eric and Patrick again. And I'm back in Kilbitè, this time only for an hour. But in God's economy, an hour can have the value of eternity.

You know you've got redneck DNA when you say, "Watch this."

Watch this …

I asked my group if we could stop by the village and see Guinel. They obliged. We gifted Guinel and his village with a portable water-filtration device. After being in Kilbitè and seeing Guinel again, I was certain I had to come back.

Now fast forward again. A year later, I put together a medical team. We traveled to Haiti to minister in Kilbitè.

The sight of a Band-Aid makes me faint, so I wasn't much use to the medical team. I knew, however, that I had a unique opportunity to speak to Guinel once again. So, while the team was setting up, Guinel and I went for a walk. He gave me a tour deep into the village jungle.

Here we were, two men who lived thousands of miles

apart and spoke no common language. Yet there was a sense between us that we were kindred spirits.

I was pleased to go deeper in the Haitian jungle. Mango trees were everywhere. The spiritual adventure was thrilling. The vegetation was thick. The path was narrow. With Eric as our translator, we talked as we walked single file on the jungle path.

I was always liked walking and talking with friends. This would turn out to be one of the most memorable walk-and-talks of my life.

Guinel and I were getting to know one another. This was the first time we ever had a personal conversation with real depth. The first two times we met, we talked briefly, yet we knew we could be pals.

As we headed back toward the village, I asked Guinel, "Are you a Christian?"

His answer wasn't surprising. "No. I'm not good enough to be a Christian."

Those were his exact words.

We were just talking. I wasn't preaching, just engaging in simple dialogue. I told Guinel that Jesus lived a perfect life. I told him our righteousness doesn't save us, but Jesus's righteousness does. And that if he put his faith in Jesus, He would give him perfect righteousness.

I told him Jesus would give him spiritual clothes: the perfect white robes of righteousness. That way, when Guinel stood before God to be judged, God would see him the same way He sees Jesus. Perfect. In perfect clothes. Spotless.

I wasn't thinking Guinel would be converted. I was just explaining the gospel to my new buddy.

To a Haitian, clothes are very important. In a Haitian's mind, clothes can bind you or free you. They figure if you don't have nice clothes, clean clothes, attractive-looking clothes, then you're not worth much. In fact, most Haitians have a fear of not being dressed up enough at church.

It may seem odd to Americans, but some Haitians believe they can't be a Christian if they don't have a set of really nice clothing. They assume God will not accept them. Would they come out and say this? Probably not.

Sometimes how you appear in church influences your thinking about yourself.

I couldn't help but think of the brown-paneled church. God looks at the inside.

Guinel wanted to know how God could see him this way. At that time, I knew nothing about clothes in the Haitian culture. He wanted more details about this divine clothing.

I told him that when he accepted Jesus by faith, God would gift him with perfectly white robes. Like the robe Jesus wears in Heaven. Jesus earned this robe by living a perfect life. He was good enough. He was willing to give the gift of His righteousness, His perfect clothing to any would who would accept Him by faith.

Again, I thought we were just talking.

What happened next took me totally by surprise. As we continued down the jungle path, Guinel started shaking and fighting back tears. Then he wept. Hard. This lasted for about a hundred steps as we came upon the stream that ran through the village.

Years earlier the government had built this concrete

canal, two to four feet wide at any given point.

Turns out it would be a miles-long baptistery.

Guinel's response seemed strange to me. I didn't know him all that well. Was he always emotional like this? What was going on here?

Back then, I did not realize how strong voodoo was in the village. Or that the gospel had never been spoken much here, if at all. And for over three hundred years, this village had never had a church, much less a Christian influence. This gospel was something Guinel had never heard. God's sacred words made Guinel shake.

The gospel message is powerful. In it, God works. And God's gospel was working hard and fast on Guinel. We were right next to the stream that flowed through the village. Really gross water. I didn't know it at the time, but that stream contained cholera, and many village people have died because of it. It was about three feet wide and about two feet deep where we stood. I told Guinel that, if he accepted Jesus by faith, he should be baptized to show God he was serious about his confession and faith. He didn't hesitate.

It all happened so fast, I just went with it.

I also didn't know that Haitian culture takes baptism very seriously. Or that Guinel's immediate plunge into the water was also very unusual.

We knelt in the water while Guinel asked questions about how God accepts him. He was still very emotional. When I told him about the Holy Spirit and God's forgiveness, he shook even harder. I told him about the cross. About Jesus' blood and how it washes us. Much like a stream can clean us.

When I mentioned to Guinel that Jesus was alive, he started crying again and dropped his face into his hands. I asked if he would pray in his own words to receive Jesus. He did.

I then baptized Guinel.

The Holy Spirit did deep and powerful work that day. I marveled, watching Him move upon Guinel so decisively. It was as if he was in the hand of God. God went straight to Guinel's heart and showed him powerful truths. And then graced him to believe.

It was as if God had led me straight to Guinel with His words and then led Guinel straight into that water. It was supernatural!

I had been sent to meet Guinel. I figured that out two years after we first met.

God taught me many things over long periods of time, and I didn't realize it until I'd gone much further down the road. I had no idea something much larger was going on. On this Haitian journey, God again revealed to me His heart for multiplication.

Through Guinel, God reminded me how essential discipleship is to the Kingdom. When God gives me two, He wants a return of four. Five and a return of ten. God had been repeating this lesson to me ever since He made me a Christian.

We often can't see our spiritual markers until we look back. Many of my lessons about discipleship started when I was in jail ministry. These were good foundations.

My friend Sue was my first mentor in jail ministry. She was the Prison Fellowship leader at the county jail and she lived discipleship. She took me under her wing.

Taught me the ropes. She also gave me opportunities to grow through some real boneheaded mistakes.

Discipleship happens when the student makes mistakes and the teacher teaches the student through those mistakes.

Here's a lesson I learned by making a mistake: Never give a convict your spiritual mentor's phone number. Sorry, Sue.

Much of my time in jail ministry was about the do's and don'ts of discipleship. Me being discipled by Sue. Me discipling inmates.

After five years of jail ministry I did five years of prison ministry. Sue later reminded me that prison ministry was cross-cultural training for Haiti. And I didn't even have to leave the country. Sue sees the Kingdom really well. It took me a while, however.

My friendship with Sue was a spiritual marker.

Looking back at those days, I see that I just wasn't adding discipleship to evangelism. At least not with the kind of momentum God desires.

Because I had to move hours away to be a prison chaplain, my discipleship under Sue faded. I had fewer opportunities to mimic Sue as my mentor.

My learning curve was getting steep.

And I wasn't connecting the dots.

During my prison ministry years, I was alone. I had no mentor.

Also, until this point, much of my Christian experience revolved around mercy and evangelism, as you've read in my stories. But realizing how discipleship fits into the Kingdom of God—not so much. Not like it should have been.

From the brown paneled church until Haiti, I connected the dots only a little at a time to see how critical discipleship is to His Kingdom puzzle.

God to Jeff: Find this man. Lead him to Me. Disciple him.

Guinel would be the man God sent me two thousand miles to find.

To lead him before the throne of grace.

And then to disciple him.

A real problem in the village is the number of men who abandon their women and children. Kilbitè has about two hundred households. Fewer than twenty of them include a married mom and dad.

Biblical discipleship is critically important for every culture.

So when I met Guinel, one of the first items on the table was teaching him Biblical responsibility. Commit to caring for your girlfriend and kids and go about it as if God is the most important person in your life. Get married, you knucklehead!

Guinel is not a totally stiff-necked redneck. It took him only five years to tie the knot.

I learned patience in this process as well.

Discipleship is contagious. As I discipled Guinel, I also discipled his girlfriend, Anid. And as I taught this couple, other couples in the church watched closely.

Guinel and Anid were the first couple in Kilbitè to marry in the church. Five years after his conversion, I was best man at Guinel's wedding. And on their wedding day, I baptized Anid as well. She had been converted just a month earlier and requested to be baptized on her wedding day.

Others were being discipled in the village while this was going on. The next year there was a triple wedding in the village.

Discipleship is indeed like being married. Sacrifice and humility are required.

Still, I needed more clarity to explain discipleship. This is what I came up with after watching Jesus teach His disciples.

*I do. You watch.*
*You do. I watch.*
*We do.*
*Wash. Rinse. Repeat.*

Guinel and I both worked hard at being a good student and a good teacher. We are also both dreamers. Our big plans were for the Kingdom of God in Kilbitè to overflow. To multiply. We share a passion for people.

So it didn't take long for visions of church planting to show up on our radar screens.

Watch this:

Over the past eight years, Guinel and I started a church together. Then we built a church building. Then we got more folks coming to church. Then we expanded the church building.

Then we started a school. Then we built a school building. Our elementary school in the Haitian jungle has eighty-four students. The church over a hundred folks. Guinel is now an ordained deacon in the church.

God's fruit through discipleship.

Guinel's wife, Anid, had a dream the day after we

finished the church building. That first church had no siding and a dirt floor, with only a roof to keep the sun off us. In her dream, she stood at the end of the church and watched as God covered the sides of the building and the dirt floor and the shoddy benches with bright white linens. A voice told her, "This is for My worship."

The Christians in Kilbitè named our church The Church of the God of Perfection.

When Guinel heard about the dream of the clean white linens, he remembered his conversion. For Guinel, that dream helped him connect the dots and recognize God's Kingdom.

He recognized God's perfection expressing itself through his life. That's humbling. Through the church. That's exciting. Through the school. That's application. All through the providence of God. That's His Kingdom.

Discipleship happens. And when it does, the Kingdom of God grows exponentially.

It was definitely worth looking for.

## *Connecting the Dots*

- The gospel Guinel heard was the great exchange. God saves us through His righteousness instead of our measly attempts at righteousness. On the cross, Jesus took our sin. Then He gave us His righteousness. When we accept this by faith, God sees us clothed in the righteousness of Jesus. This is the gospel.

- God made him who had no sin to be sin for us, so that in him we might become the righteousness of God. (2 Corinthians 5:21 NIV)

- How much more will those who receive God's abundant provision of grace and of the gift of righteousness reign in life through the one man, Jesus Christ! (Romans 5:17 NIV)

- What is more, I consider everything a loss because of the surpassing worth of knowing Christ Jesus my Lord, for whose sake I have lost all things. I consider them garbage, that I may gain Christ and be found in him, not having a righteousness of my own that comes from the law, but that which is through faith in Christ—the righteousness that comes from God on the basis of faith. (Philippians 3:8-9 NIV)

- Later I passed by, and when I looked at you and saw that you were old enough for love, I spread the corner of my garment over you and covered your naked body. I gave you my solemn oath and entered into a covenant with you, declares the Sovereign Lord, and you became mine. I bathed you with water and washed the blood from you and put ointments on you.

> I clothed you with an embroidered dress and put sandals of fine leather on you. I dressed you in fine linen and covered you with costly garments. I adorned you with jewelry: I put bracelets on your arms and a necklace around your neck, and I put a ring on your nose, earrings on your ears and a beautiful crown on your head. So you were adorned with gold and silver; your clothes were of fine linen and costly fabric and embroidered cloth. Your food was honey, olive oil and the finest flour. You became very beautiful and rose to be a queen. And your fame spread among the nations on account of your beauty, because the splendor I had given you made your beauty perfect, declares the Sovereign Lord. (Ezekiel 16:8-14 NIV)

Guinel accepted by faith what God promised to do for him. That was his salvation. Then he started on the road to becoming a disciple of Jesus.

- Being a disciple of Jesus is hard work. So is discipling others. Jesus showed us the perfect pattern of discipleship.

- "Very truly I tell you, the Son can do nothing by himself; he can do only what he sees his Father doing, because whatever the Father does the Son also does." (John 5:19 NIV)

- A disciple has many roles in God's Kingdom. Above all else, the disciple of Jesus is to be a servant.

- Jesus called them together and said, "You know that the rulers of the Gentiles lord it over them, and their high officials exercise authority over them. Not so with you. Instead, whoever wants to become great among you must be your servant, and whoever wants to be first must be your slave—just as the Son of Man did not come to be served, but to serve, and to give his life as a ransom for many." (Matthew 20:25-28 NIV)

- God's disciple is like a soldier and understands the chain of command. God is the One giving the orders. The disciple is subordinate.

- No one serving as a soldier gets entangled in civilian affairs, but rather tries to please his commanding officer. (2 Timothy 2:4 NIV)

- His disciple is to be like a soldier sent on a mission with a dispatch: a message proclaiming Christ.

- That which was from the beginning, which we have heard, which we have seen with our eyes, which we have looked at and our hands have touched—this we proclaim concerning the Word of life. (1 John 1:1 NIV)

- A servant. A soldier. A messenger. An ambassador.

- Paul says, "Pray also for me, that whenever I speak, words may be given me so that I will fearlessly make known the mystery of the gospel, for which I am an ambassador in chains. Pray that I may declare [proclaim] it fearlessly, as I should." (Ephesians 6:19-20 NIV)

- The goal of our roles for the sake of the Kingdom of God? Multiplication.
- "Again, it will be like a man going on a journey, who called his servants and entrusted his wealth to them. To one he gave five bags of gold, to another two bags, and to another one bag, each according to his ability. Then he went on his journey. The man who had received five bags of gold went at once and put his money to work and gained five bags more. So also, the one with two bags of gold gained two more. But the man who had received one bag went off, dug a hole in the ground and hid his master's money.

After a long time the master of those servants returned and settled accounts with them.

The man who had received five bags of gold brought the other five. 'Master,' he said, 'you entrusted me with five bags of gold. See, I have gained five more.'

His master replied, 'Well done, good and faithful servant! You have been faithful with a few things; I will put you in charge of many things. Come and share your master's happiness!' "The man with the two talents also came. 'Master,' he said, 'you entrusted me with two talents; see, I have gained two more.'" His master replied, 'Well done, good and faithful servant! You have been faithful with a few things; I will put you in charge of many things. Come and share your master's happiness!'

Then the man who had received one bag of gold came. 'Master,' he said, 'I knew that you are a hard man, harvesting where you have not sown and gathering where you have not scattered seed. So I was afraid and went out and hid your gold in the ground. See, here is what belongs to you.'

His master replied, 'You wicked, lazy servant! So you knew that I harvest where I have not sown and gather where I have not scattered seed? Well then, you should have put my money on deposit with the bankers, so that when I returned I would have received it back with interest.

So take the bag of gold from him and give it to the one who has ten bags. For whoever has will be given more, and they will have an abundance. Whoever does not have, even what they have will be taken from them. And throw that worthless servant outside, into the darkness, where there will be weeping and gnashing of teeth.'" (Matthew 25:14-30 NIV)

Therefore go and make disciples of all nations, baptizing them in the name of the Father and of the Son and of the Holy Spirit, and teaching them to obey everything I have commanded you. And surely I am with you always, to the very end of the age. (Matthew 28:19-20 NIV)

## Chapter 12
## Let the Chunks Fall Where They May

A man can't walk away from his own story.

Sometimes your own story reveals the reason for your story. What's really nuts is when your story tells you which path to take.

Who's writing this story, anyway? Turns out it's God. It's not my script. It's His. He is the Author and Director of my screenplay. A photo album of snapshots from a renegade redneck evangelist.

It took fifty-nine years, seven months, and twenty-one days for me to figure out the purpose of my life. His story. I started out clueless. Got a few nuggets along the way. But when the final piece came together in a jungle in Haiti, it showed me just how much purpose was embedded in all those previous assignments.

I'm not going to connect the dots in this chapter with Bible verses as I have in the previous chapters. This time I'm going to use a bird's-eye view to connect thirty-one years' worth of spiritual dots to one grand purpose.

Fairy tales start with, "Once upon a time."

Redneck tales start with, "Hold my beer and watch this."

Because I was a knucklehead with an attitude problem (don't even try to look surprised), I had been through my share of bosses. Gary, though, was different. Gary was probably the best boss I ever had. I sold advertising space for his growing billboard business. He was a sharp businessman. He was good for me. His purpose was profit and I respected that. He genuinely cared for my success.

I made Gary a ton of money for his business. But the poor guy had to deal with my self-serving attitude.

One day Gary had to call me into his office to give me the what-for. In short, he told me I acted as if I thought the rules didn't apply to me. I was quick enough and devious enough to fake some humility and lower my head in shame. But inside I was thinking, "Duh, Gary! Of course the rules don't apply to me!" My second thought was, "Rules? What rules?"

Gary was right. I played by Jeff's rules. He identified something in me I was oblivious to.

I worked for Gary in my early thirties. That was the time of life when God saved me. It would still take me decades to figure out the reason for my story. The story He planned.

You have to crack a few eggs to find out what's inside. No one ever completely gets over being a knucklehead on this side of glory. And still, at this point in life, I had no idea I was living my story as if it was all about me.

Just ask my wife and kids and friends. For Jeff, life was all about Jeff. I was the reason for everything I did. And that's ugly.

A famous Brit once said something like, "When you're twenty, you care what everyone thinks about you. By the time you're forty, you stop caring what everyone thinks, and when you're sixty, you realize no one was ever thinking about you in the first place."

I got it all backward. Up until I was forty, I didn't give a rip what anyone thought about what I did or how I looked doing it.

Somebody once said our lives start out like a big chunk of marble. And as we age, God is like a sculptor. He shapes us to be like Him. He starts with a jackhammer. Then a sledgehammer. Then a hammer and a chisel to shape us. And then in Heaven, where we're all finished, we're like His shiny sculpture, polished with a jeweler's cloth.

As the years went on, you could hear chunks of my marble hitting the floor.

When I was forty, I went to seminary. That's when God starting using a jackhammer on me. I'll give the Lord credit. It was a quiet jackhammer. Effective too. He broke off just the right pieces at the right time. His jackhammer was measured and precise.

My wife might disagree. She was hoping God would use a wrecking ball.

Seminary opened up a whole new world to me. It was like a three-year Bible study with really hard tests and papers to write. But I loved it. There I learned how to read and write, to understand what God had been saying to me through the years.

He started giving me reasons for living, other than myself.

Every day, seminary was like watching a rerun of Star Trek. It showed me the perfect blend of logic and mystery. There I began to discover that I needed to take some steps to dismantle my arrogance. To boldly go ...

At seminary I discovered: 1) I had a story. 2) My story needed changing.

My story was not *by* Jeff alone, *through* Jeff alone, *in*

Jeff alone.

I was impressed with the Sangre de Cristo Seminary. They got right to business. On the very first day, they showed me an ancient book full of questions and answers. Not being a Presbyterian by birth, I was unfamiliar with the mysteries it explained. Still, I knew enough to know it was valuable, since it was written centuries ago by a bunch of dead Presbyterians.

The first question the dead Presbyterians asked was: What is the chief end of man? Their answer? Man's chief end is to glorify God and enjoy Him forever.

I was in a room full of seminary students when I heard this for the first time. It was as if beams of light came bursting through solid walls and rested on me. Like an earthquake that shook me while everyone else sat motionless.

It was an epiphany of epiphanies. I couldn't believe what I had just read. Was anybody else getting this? Here it was—the meaning of life in just seven words. And in print, no less.

I think I found my special purpose: to glorify God and enjoy Him forever.

Living life to enjoy and glorify God? I felt as if I was in a redneck beer commercial in a spiritual context. It didn't get any better than this.

It figures this would be the type of answer I had looked for all my life. Simple and yet profound. Like water shallow enough for a child to play in, yet deep enough for an elephant to swim in.

My purpose was becoming clearer. But I still had some chunks of marble that needed hammering.

All my life, I've cried out to God, "What do you want?" His answer was always the same. "I want you, Jeff." Sometimes I hated that answer. Other times it drove me to my knees in prayer. Lord, can't You be specific? This is Your gig. I need more clarity here, Lord.

After my seminary epiphany, I started redirecting my life, based on the revelations of those dead Presbyterians.

Years after seminary, when I was in my early fifties, I went with my buddy Greg to our annual pastors' conference. That's when God used blasting caps to knock off another chunk of marble. Just ask Greg. He will tell you that watching more marble hit the floor was both painful to watch and glorious to behold.

When God gets through to folks, it's usually messy and emotional before the phoenix.

At the end of each conference, it was the tradition to have a man speak about missions. I don't remember who he was, but this guy was good.

He talked about what God wanted. And when he said he kept crying out to God, asking Him what He wanted, I tuned in.

Everyone at this conference had given their lives to the Lord in ministry. But this guy was asking us to give more to God. More? What more could I give to God than what I was already giving?

The marble cracked. Ready to fall.

The speaker said folks put 10 percent of their earnings in the offering plate. Now, take that concept and apply it to your life. What about giving 10 percent of your life to missions?

*You mean like seven years of my life in the offering plate?* Enter the Holy Spirit.

To me, the speaker's message made no sense. Why would I give seven years to missions? To His mission? To His story? It seemed like a rip-off. A cheat. God would be getting the short end of things. Didn't He deserve all of me? All my time? If I understood my salvation properly, I was going to get eternity, but I'm going to give Him only seven years of missions from a seventy-year life?

When I was in prison ministry, I was a missionary. I had to scare up my paychecks by asking for money. Some missionaries call that sharing the vision. It was both. Sacrificing for Jesus got to me. Made me tired, even resentful. If I was going to work for Jesus, I needed a regular paycheck. After all, there was a limit to what I was willing to sacrifice for Him.

But that's not what the Holy Spirit had been saying to me. That is not what Jesus meant when He said, "Follow Me." He made it clear he wanted all of me in that collection plate. From an eternal perspective, He told me to give it all up for Him. Go for it.

So I did.

That's when things took a turn for the better, spiritually speaking. I found more joy. More suffering. More faith. More satisfaction, even though I was making less money. Considering the cross of Christ ... this makes perfect sense.

My anger, arrogance, and selfishness were being chipped away.

At this conference I also heard a familiar mantra. I'd read these words before and had heard them many times at previous conferences. This concept was a shiny nugget, more valuable than gold. A nugget that would change me and alter my story. It helped me connect the dots.

It goes like this: God is most glorified in us when we are most satisfied in Him.

This felt like a spiritual gut check. A clear way to put my faith in perspective. Brilliant!

The first four life chunks of marble to fall were essential to getting a handle on my/His story.

1. I did not choose God. He chose me.

2. Grace alone. Faith alone. Christ alone.

3. To glorify God and enjoy Him forever.

4. God is most glorified in us when we are most satisfied in Him.

Hmm. We're getting closer here.

59 years, 7 months, and 21 days, and another chunk of marble hits the floor.

The Haitian jungle can be a spiritually cleansing place.

My Haitian ministry was growing and doing well. The school in the village could handle way more kids than the eighty-four we have now. So what to do? Stand pat? Trust God and build a bigger school?

My buddy Steve is one of the choicest rednecks you'll ever meet. Common sense oozes out of this guy. He's a real warrior for Jesus. He houses ex-cons, future cons, immigrants, welfare moms, you name it. This guy has a heart of gold.

We were having breakfast when he told me that through his Bible reading, he felt certain that God wanted him to throw a party. Not just any party. A huge worship celebration. A blowout. And he wanted to do it for the church and village in Kilbitè.

Steve would pay for my travel to Haiti to throw this party. To feed four hundred people. To buy Bibles. Hire a worship band. He was going all out for the worship of God.

"Yeah, Steve, worship is great and everything, but how about we take that money and start construction on the new school?"

Steve would have none of it. His gift must be used to worship God. To give God all the credit for what He had done in Steve's life. In mine. In the lives of the village.

That's when it hit me. My buddy was giving money to worship God. And I was arguing with him. It didn't take me long to hear my own words. Seriously? I'm arguing with someone who wants to give me thousands of dollars to help that Haitian village and church worship God? What a knucklehead!

That piece of marble left a noticeable dent when it crashed.

Jeff: "Hey, God, what do You want?

God: I want you, Jeff. I want to be listened to. I want to be believed. I want to be obeyed. I want to be worshipped.

Worship.

That's it! That is what my story is about. He sent me to fetch folks to worship Him.

All those nerds, rednecks, and knuckleheads I shared

the gospel with were put in God's crosshairs so they would worship Him.

Just think, I figured this out in under six decades. I think that's pretty good. Some folks never get it.

We used that worship service, which Steve paid for, as a celebration of God's goodness in launching the building of our new school.

It was an incredible scene. We set up a makeshift stage in a clearing in the Haitian jungle, surrounded by plantains, banana plants, and mango trees. We powered everything with generators. We fed over four hundred villagers. Hundreds of people were there, worshipping. Praying, singing, and preaching lasted most of the day.

About halfway through my sermon, a young man seated in back raised his hand and kept it raised for the last half of my message. He was trying desperately to make eye contact with me the entire time.

When my sermon was over, he ran to the front. He said he didn't want to talk to me, but rather to everyone there. This guy wanted the microphone, and he couldn't wait any longer. He had to tell everyone what had just happened. He said until this day he never could talk about Jesus. But not this day! This day he confessed to everyone his new faith and salvation.

He told me personally that this was the first time in his life he had ever worshipped God.

Next Sunday he was early at church to worship.

God is poetic. On our special worship celebration day, He demonstrated not only His purpose, but the purpose for Christians. He did so through the words and worship of that young man.

Steve sent me to Haiti to learn about the priority of worship. Then God used the salvation of that young man as a living object lesson to drive home His lesson to me: God has a passion for His worship. God understands His glory. He knows better than anyone the worship that is due Him.

God could not have been clearer to me. He demonstrated His purpose personally to me, through a friend and through a stranger. It was humbling. Affirming. Motivating.

There are many things on this earth that we won't see in Heaven: worry, ill health, comparing ourselves to our neighbors, stress, hassles, annoyances, people who get on our nerves. No one will need to repent there. We'll have no stupid decisions, no confusion, no conflicts. But there will be one carryover from here to there.

Worship.

Jesus told His disciples to "Go!" He was sending them to fetch souls. Souls to worship Him forever in Heaven. Worship due Him. Worship because of all His grace, mercy, and goodness.

It makes perfect sense. The reason God had me evangelize all those people for all those years was so they would worship Him.

He is the Author of my story. The main Character of my story. The purpose of my story. He is the means and the end of my story. He is Who my story points to.

Nobody tells a better story than Jesus.

My spiritual story started way before the brown-paneled church. It was written before that knuckleheaded altar boy spilled the communion wine.

Before I was born. Before the earth was even made. Every story starts in the heart of God.

No amount of time, nor any knucklehead, has the power to bind His goodness or the worship due Him.

And if someone looks long enough and hard enough, through the eyes of faith, they can see how God connects the dots for every nerd, redneck, and knucklehead.

## A note to the reader:

Thank you for purchasing and reading this book. All the proceeds from the sales of this book go to support God's Mercy to Haiti. We are a non-profit teaching and mercy ministry to the impoverished Haitian village of Kilbite, Haiti.

Please visit our website at
www.godsmercytohaiti.org